# GEOPOLITICS OF U.S. OIL AND GAS COMPETITIVENESS

## HEARING

BEFORE THE

SUBCOMMITTEE ON TERRORISM,
NONPROLIFERATION, AND TRADE

OF THE

## COMMITTEE ON FOREIGN AFFAIRS
## HOUSE OF REPRESENTATIVES

ONE HUNDRED FIFTEENTH CONGRESS

SECOND SESSION

MAY 22, 2018

**Serial No. 115–132**

Printed for the use of the Committee on Foreign Affairs

Available: http://www.foreignaffairs.house.gov/, http://docs.house.gov,
or http://www.gpo.gov/fdsys/

U.S. GOVERNMENT PUBLISHING OFFICE

30–173PDF  WASHINGTON : 2018

COMMITTEE ON FOREIGN AFFAIRS

EDWARD R. ROYCE, California, *Chairman*

CHRISTOPHER H. SMITH, New Jersey
ILEANA ROS-LEHTINEN, Florida
DANA ROHRABACHER, California
STEVE CHABOT, Ohio
JOE WILSON, South Carolina
MICHAEL T. McCAUL, Texas
TED POE, Texas
DARRELL E. ISSA, California
TOM MARINO, Pennsylvania
MO BROOKS, Alabama PAUL
COOK, California SCOTT
PERRY, Pennsylvania RON
DeSANTIS, Florida
MARK MEADOWS, North Carolina
TED S. YOHO, Florida
ADAM KINZINGER, Illinois
LEE M. ZELDIN, New York
DANIEL M. DONOVAN, Jr., New York
F. JAMES SENSENBRENNER, Jr., Wisconsin
ANN WAGNER, Missouri
BRIAN J. MAST, Florida
FRANCIS ROONEY, Florida
BRIAN K. FITZPATRICK, Pennsylvania
THOMAS A. GARRETT, Jr., Virginia
JOHN R. CURTIS, Utah

ELIOT L. ENGEL, New York
BRAD SHERMAN, California
GREGORY W. MEEKS, New York
ALBIO SIRES, New Jersey
GERALD E. CONNOLLY, Virginia
THEODORE E. DEUTCH, Florida
KAREN BASS, California
WILLIAM R. KEATING, Massachusetts
DAVID N. CICILLINE, Rhode Island
AMI BERA, California
LOIS FRANKEL, Florida
TULSI GABBARD, Hawaii
JOAQUIN CASTRO, Texas
ROBIN L. KELLY, Illinois
BRENDAN F. BOYLE, Pennsylvania
DINA TITUS, Nevada
NORMA J. TORRES, California
BRADLEY SCOTT SCHNEIDER, Illinois
THOMAS R. SUOZZI, New York
ADRIANO ESPAILLAT, New York
TED LIEU, California

AMY PORTER, *Chief of Staff*　　THOMAS SHEEHY, *Staff Director*
JASON STEINBAUM, *Democratic Staff Director*

---

SUBCOMMITTEE ON TERRORISM, NONPROLIFERATION, AND TRADE

TED POE, Texas, *Chairman*

JOE WILSON, South Carolina
DARRELL E. ISSA, California
PAUL COOK, California
SCOTT PERRY, Pennsylvania
LEE M. ZELDIN, New York
BRIAN J. MAST, Florida
THOMAS A. GARRETT, Jr., Virginia

WILLIAM R. KEATING, Massachusetts
LOIS FRANKEL, Florida
BRENDAN F. BOYLE, Pennsylvania
DINA TITUS, Nevada
NORMA J. TORRES, California
BRADLEY SCOTT SCHNEIDER, Illinois

# CONTENTS

Page

## WITNESSES

Kenneth B. Medlock III, Ph.D., senior director, Center for Energy Studies, Baker Institute for Public Policy, Rice University .......................................... 5
Mr. David Carroll, president and chief executive officer, Gas Technology Institute ................................................................................................................ 19
Ms. Sarah Ladislaw, director and senior fellow, Energy and National Security Program, Center for Strategic and International Studies ................................ 29
Ms. Samantha Gross, fellow, Cross-Brookings Initiative on Energy and Climate, The Brookings Institution ........................................................................ 38

## LETTERS, STATEMENTS, ETC., SUBMITTED FOR THE HEARING

Kenneth B. Medlock III, Ph.D.: Prepared statement .......................................... 8
Mr. David Carroll: Prepared statement ............................................................... 21
Ms. Sarah Ladislaw: Prepared statement ............................................................ 32
Ms. Samantha Gross: Prepared statement .......................................................... 40

## APPENDIX

Hearing notice ........................................................................................................ 54
Hearing minutes .................................................................................................... 55

# GEOPOLITICS OF U.S. OIL AND GAS COMPETITIVENESS

## TUESDAY, MAY 22, 2018

House of Representatives,
Subcommittee on Terrorism, Nonproliferation, and Trade,
Committee on Foreign Affairs,
*Washington, DC.*

The subcommittee met, pursuant to notice, at 2 o'clock p.m., in room 2200 Rayburn House Office Building, Hon. Ted Poe (chairman of the subcommittee) presiding.

Mr. POE. This is a rectangular gavel but it ought to work.

The subcommittee will come to order. Without objection, all members will have 3 days—5 days, rather—to submit statements, questions, and extraneous materials for the record, subject to the length limitation in the rules.

The U.S. oil and gas industry is a force multiplier for American influence around the world. For decades, many of the planet's great energy producers were regimes ruled by tyrants who leveraged their oil wealth to oppress their own people and pursue evil foreign policy.

However, thanks to American know-how, the United States has unleashed its own energy potential, now becoming a major player in the global market—I should say, the major player.

In large part, America's revival as an energy superpower is a result of the shale revolution. Through the process of hydraulic fracturing—or fracking, as it is called, which was invented in the '40s and expanded recently to be more efficient—we are now able to reach oil and gas deep within the earth, where they were previously unreachable.

With this new technology, the U.S. has gone from the world's largest oil importer to one of the world's largest energy exporters. The United States primarily imports heavy crude oil and exports light crude—Texas sweet crude, as we call it.

Just a decade ago, the U.S. was importing 12.5 million barrels per day of crude oil and fuel, and now it's just 4 billion.

Between 2010 and 2017, oil production rose from 5 million barrels per day to 10 million barrels a day, approaching a record last set in 1970.

This has allowed for a dramatic reduction of our dependence on foreign oil, which ultimately strengthens our national security. The United States has been talking about being energy independent since I was born. I am glad to see that we are finally getting to that point.

In the nearly 3 years since Congress ended restrictions on exporting crude oil, the U.S. has beat market expectations and surged its exports to a record 2.5 million barrels, and by 2022 we will export more oil than we import.

Some people wonder why we export and import both oils. The United States uses heavy crude in its refineries, and it's too expensive to switch from heavy crude to light crude.

So we import our heavy crude and then we export the light crude that other nations use that we develop quite rapidly.

Also, we have natural gas production that has been setting new records in every year since 2000 thanks to the innovations of liquefied natural gas——LNG, as we call it. We ship this growing resource anywhere in the world.

Last year, we became a net exporter of natural gas for the first time in 60 years. In the coming years, it will only improve as the market of natural gas consumers grows and more exporting facilities come online.

America's comeback as an energy superpower has wide-ranging geopolitical implications besides the economic benefits to the United States and other countries.

Its obvious benefit for Americans and the U.S. economy is that it reduces our trade balance and creates new well-paying jobs and it also generates more revenue, making us a stronger nation.

But it also means less money that is going into repressive regimes all over the world who were previously dependent—we were dependent on for oil, and since energy is more abundant, the price of oil is decreasing.

Overall, the result is less money for Putin's Russia, the Ayatollah's Iran, and Maduro's Venezuela—all totalitarian regimes that oppress their people and make their living by selling oil and gas.

With the low price of oil, international sanctions, and their own economic mismanagement, these regimes, who could rely on their oil wealth to fund their activities—their nefarious activities—are instead seeking their economic—or sinking in their economic tank.

Now the people are on the streets demanding accountability, and Saudi Arabia and the Gulf States have long been important partners of the U.S. because we needed their oil and their leverage in stabilizing oil prices.

Now we can redefine our relationship with those countries as well. This does not mean we should become isolationists or abandon our traditional partners. It just means we should work better.

We have oil, we have natural gas, and we need to give the Europeans an alternative to the blackmail from Russia and Russia's natural gas, especially Eastern Europe.

Several years ago, I was in Ukraine in the winter, and the Russians turned off the gas. It was dark, it was cold, and people died, and they did it for political reasons—to try to put their muscle on Ukraine, which they are still trying to do.

But that's just one example of the way the Russians use natural gas as a way to force other countries to deal with them politically.

U.S. oil and gas exports also reinforce the importance of free trade. I am a free trader. I think we should—that includes NAFTA but we need to make NAFTA fair and free trade as well, which talks are going on now.

About 60 percent of U.S. gas exports go to Mexico, which provide a major boost to our trade balance, and Canada has also become a major importer of America-refined fuels.

I have long thought that the United States—the four countries of Canada, United States, Texas, and Mexico—should work together to have a North American alliance on energy.

We could become the energy major player in the world on all types of energy if we just worked a little bit more together to make sure that we can use that as an economic advantage but also as a geopolitical tool against these totalitarian regimes.

So I am looking forward to hearing what our witnesses have to say on these issues, give us some insight, and also if there are things that Congress needs to do or not do to make sure that the United States continues its energy exploration.

I will now turn to my friend from Massachusetts, Mr. Keating, for his opening statement and comments.

Mr. KEATING. Thank you, Mr. Chairman, and thank you for letting us all know your true beliefs that Texas is a sovereign country. It's something we suspected.

Mr. POE. You didn't know that? [Laughter.]

Mr. KEATING. Well, I do now. I know it now. So I'll bring that message back to Massachusetts.

I would like to thank the chairman for convening today's hearing. This is an important topic because there are a lot of factors that make development efforts more effective and enhance our national and global security.

However, there are fewer things that, without them, there simply cannot be development or economic growth and adequate levels of security would be really impossible to achieve and energy is one of those things.

U.S. oil and gas exports—the topic of our hearing today—are an interesting piece of the global energy puzzle and shouldn't be considered lightly—both in terms of the possible impact on our own energy policy and national security and also on those of many other countries as well.

With the decision to export oil and natural gas, we also have the opportunity to be highly strategic in thinking about our energy export policies and the geopolitical context they create.

For example, some European countries have considered importing U.S. LNG to reduce their reliance on Russia to meet their energy needs.

While we are facing Russia's destabilizing interventions around the world, including our own democratic elections here in the United States, we have to pay attention to shifts like this that open up new opportunities to promote our own strategic interests abroad.

In fact, energy was one sector proposed for inclusion in the now-stalled Transatlantic Trade and Investment Partnership with the E.U.—with the idea of bringing lower barriers to exporting U.S. oil and gas to our friends and allies in Europe.

Additionally, two of our largest LNG customers are Canada and Mexico. If the President does in fact withdraw from NAFTA, that will have a big effect on the sector and on thousands of jobs that support this industry here in the United States.

Even my own sovereign country, Massachusetts, which is not an oil or natural gas-producing state, supports—we support these industries with manufacturing and service sectors and contribute a significant percentage of labor income to the crude oil supply chain here in the United States.

Our oil and gas export policy has the potential to shape the lives of countless Americans not only in daily economic terms here but also in how we are ultimately impacted—how we are impacted by the effects of our export policies abroad.

Just as we cannot be blind to the countless economic and geopolitical implications of our U.S. oil and gas export policy, we must also be vigilant about putting this policy in context.

In a post-Paris Climate Agreement world, there is a nearly universal commitment to addressing the impacts of climate change.

Investments in clean energy and renewables will be a big part of that, not just for the U.S. and other countries but for developing economies as well.

The effects of global markets for oil and gas should also be part of our conversation about the makeup of U.S. energy exports.

What will be the breakdown of our energy exports? How much will oil and gas be a part of that? How much will renewable energy be part of that?

We are already seeing the reverse of this here in the United States. In my district in New Bedford, Massachusetts, Danish companies are involved in the development of wind energy in what will be one of the biggest offshore wind energy projects in the country.

Energy is a global issue. This could be a boon for American workers and American households and companies looking to have a consistent and affordable energy year round to heat and cool their homes and, importantly, to grow their businesses, or it could be a series of missed opportunities.

Our conversation today highlights oil and gas. However, it would be a mistake to ignore how these different sources of energy fit together to provide security and reliable economic growth and to ignore the inevitable long-term trajectories of our energy policies.

In choosing to export oil and gas, we have opened up a world of opportunities for interacting with other countries, global markets, conflicts, and even foreign policy considerations that go along with it.

However, that still means we must evaluate this policy in the context of our own energy and economic priorities, our long-term security interests and the realities of the foreign policy challenges that we face.

With that, Mr. Chairman, I will yield back.

Mr. POE. I thank the gentleman from Massachusetts.

The chair recognizes the gentleman from California, Mr. Rohrabacher, for an opening comment.

Mr. ROHRABACHER. Thank you very much, Mr. Chairman, and we note that energy and our ability to be self-sufficient at energy or how much energy we will have to feed our economy has been a major factor for decades, and we didn't quite realize that until

America became a net importer of oil and gas a decade or several decades ago.

Before that, I mean, we didn't give it much thought, and let's just note that once it was clear that America was headed toward a shortage of oil and gas, we still had people in our country who opposed the Alaskan Pipeline.

Had they—had they been successful, Mr. Chairman, in preventing the Alaskan Pipeline because, I understand, caribou were—it was going to hurt the caribou and, of course, those predictions have proven exactly the opposite and we have more caribou.

But that fanaticism that had them opposing the Alaskan Pipeline would have had a huge negative impact on our economy and also would have made us even more vulnerable during this time period when we have been importing oil.

But we face the same kind of thing with fracking, where fanatics have opposed fracking but yet it has given us now a new self-sufficiency.

All of these things have incredible foreign policy implications as well as economic implications for our country, and we need to understand them. Thank you for holding this hearing so we will have a better understanding.

Mr. POE. I thank the gentleman from California.

I will introduce our witnesses and, without objection, all witnesses' prepared statements will be made part of the record.

Please keep your comments and your presentation to no more than 5 minutes and I will—we will—have your presentation filed in the minutes of the hearing.

Dr. Kenneth Medlock is the senior director of the Center of Energy Studies at Rice University's Baker Institute for Public Policy. Previously, he served as vice president for conferences, United States Association for Energy Economics.

Dr. Medlock, thank you for being here and thank you for what you do at Rice University. Very good reputation.

Mr. David Carroll is the president and CEO of Gas Technology Institute. Since 2015, Mr. Carroll has also been president of the International Gas Union, which is made up of 150 member associations and corporations representing 97 percent of the global gas market.

Ms. Sarah Ladislaw is director of the Energy National Security Program at the Center for Strategic and International Studies. Previously, she worked in the Office of the Americas in the Department of Energy.

And Samantha Gross is a fellow in foreign policy at the Brookings Institute and a fellow at the Cross-Brookings Initiative on Energy and Climate.

Previously, she served as director of international climate and clean energy at the Department of Energy.

Mr. Medlock, we will start with you. Thank you.

**STATEMENT OF KENNETH B. MEDLOCK III, PH.D., SENIOR DIRECTOR, CENTER FOR ENERGY STUDIES, BAKER INSTITUTE FOR PUBLIC POLICY, RICE UNIVERSITY**

Mr. MEDLOCK. Thank you, Mr. Chairman, Mr. Keating.

I also want to thank the committee for accommodating me during the past week.

I'll take a moment just to—my grandfather passed away. He was a World War II veteran of the Navy, a member of the Mighty Midgets. For those of you who don't know history, you can look it up. It's a pretty decorated group.

He was very proud of his accomplishments but also very understated, which I think is a quality that I hope many others will emulate.

Regarding this particular testimony, shale has been utterly transformative, and that's where I want to start, because if we are going to have a conversation about U.S. soft power and U.S. foreign policy prerogative related to oil and gas, we have to acknowledge what's happened domestically on the shale front.

It has been transformative in more than just how most of us talk about it. Most of us talk about it as if there is a new source of supply that has emerged into the global market scene that's actually resulted in a reduction in import dependence in the United States.

We have seen our crude oil imports drop dramatically. We are now net exporters of natural gas as well as petroleum products or refined products.

But an important, I think, lesson in all of this, and this is really what plays into the broader discussion of what geopolitical ramifications are, if you go back to 2003, 2004, 2005, 2006, the world was really looking at the U.S. as a declining oil and gas province—a province that ultimately would continue to see declines in production, growth in demand, and increasing import dependence.

There were a lot of very significant investments made in a vertically integrated way to develop natural gas in remote parts of the world, move it through liquefaction facilities onto ships, and bring it to our shores.

Back in 2003, there were 47 different terminals that had received certification to import liquefied natural gas. Now, all of those, of course, didn't get built, but it was certainly a signal.

What drove that? Well, oftentimes we forget, and it's not that far long ago, but between 2003 and 2006, the price of natural gas in the United States was higher than anywhere else in the world.

And, of course, when you start talking about trade, you start talking about impetus for investment. At the end of the day, it really is about moving product from a low price to a high price, and that's exactly what was happening.

Of course, when you have high prices, it also stimulates other margins of response, and that's exactly what happened in the domestic upstream.

It wasn't the vertically integrated measures. It was a lot of relatively small, sometimes referred to as mom and pops, but independents that really took entrepreneurial spirit to task in the upstream.

In the Barnett Shale, for example, Mitchell Energy went in and actually started to try new things in the Fort Worth Basin, as it was previously known.

You know, drilling some vertical wells, making contact with what was known to exist for a long time—geologists had been talking about shales for decades. This is not new to a geologist.

But figuring out ways to make the resource both technically and commercially recoverable was really the big challenge. It was a challenge that was put on the table by policymakers in the late 1970s with the Eastern Gas Shales Project. It was taken onboard by various institutions including the Gas Technology Institute.

But, ultimately, what happened is you saw these high prices that matriculated into the United States, as relative demand growth and declining production resulted in significant innovation.

The key thing about the United States that I think is sometimes lost in the context of understanding what's happening domestically and what it means globally is that we enjoy a very unique set of regulatory and legal institutions in this country that have afforded us the ability to see our production grow.

It actually fosters innovation. It fosters entrepreneurial activity, and when you have that kind of environment, the sky is the limit, quite frankly.

What I just said is not unique to oil and gas, though. It's actually true across the energy value chain. So it is actually imperative that if the United States is going to continue to project its influence globally, one of the things that the U.S. Government continue to foster policies and environments that are conducive to entrepreneurial activity.

A couple of final statements along those lines—gas—what's happened here, the Marcellus is to gas what the Permian is to oil. A lot of people, I don't think, have fully internalized that.

But when we start talking about what's going to happen over the next decade in the oil space, there is—we have just begun to scratch the surface. The big issue right now is water and infrastructure.

The same thing could have been said about the Marcellus, particularly with regard to infrastructure, not too long ago. So when we look at what the Marcellus has meant for the North American natural gas scene, it's important to recognize that the Permian is likely to unveil the same sort of dramatic transformation in not only the U.S. oil market but the global oil market.

On the gas front, the U.S. now presents what we call a credible threat to Russian hegemonic intent in Europe. You've seen this in Lithuania with the construction of its natural gas import facility.

Prices were instantly negotiated once that happened because now Russia realizes there is something out there that can actually take market, and that is something that is incredibly important when you start talking about foreign policy objectives and geopolitical influence.

And the U.S. is on the cusp of actually having significant, significant impacts globally for the next several decades as a result of what's happened domestically.

I'll stop there.

[The prepared statement of Mr. Medlock follows:]

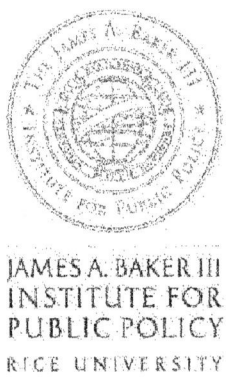

**JAMES A. BAKER III
INSTITUTE FOR
PUBLIC POLICY**
RICE UNIVERSITY

Testimony of
Kenneth B. Medlock III
James A. Baker, III, and Susan G. Baker Fellow in Energy and Resource Economics, and
Senior Director, Center for Energy Studies
James A. Baker III Institute for Public Policy
Rice University

To the
House Committee on Foreign Affairs
Subcommittee on Terrorism, Nonproliferation, and Trade

Washington, D.C.

Hearing on
Geopolitics of U.S. Oil and Gas Competitiveness

May 22, 2018

During the past 15 years, innovative new techniques involving horizontal drilling and hydraulic fracturing have unlocked a vast resource potential and resulted in the rapid growth in production of natural gas from shale. The same techniques have also matriculated into the oil sector resulting in a dramatic increase in light tight oil production. In what follows, we will address the unique set of circumstances that exist in the US that have facilitated the "era of abundance" for US oil and gas. Then, we will address the implication for energy security and how that connects to a new geopolitical reality afforded to the US, with attention given to recent changes in global oil and gas markets as evidence.

What made the successes witnessed in the US during the past 15 years possible? To begin, geology matters. The scale of the technically and economically recoverable oil and gas resources locked up in shale is tremendous and geographically diverse (see Figure 1), and as time passes the understanding of the resource expands. But, while the right geology is a *necessary* condition, it is not *sufficient*. Shale resources assessed in locations outside the US are significant, yet shale oil and gas production on a global scale is still largely limited to the US. This follows because *sufficiency* requires a host of above-ground factors to be appropriately aligned. These include market institutions and regulatory frameworks spanning the energy value chain, such as...[1]

- a regulatory and legal apparatus in which upstream firms can negotiate directly with landowners for access to mineral rights on privately-owned lands.
- a market in which liquid pricing locations, or hubs, are easily accessed due to liberalized transportation services that dictate pipeline *capacity* is unbundled from pipeline *ownership*.
- a well-developed pipeline network that can facilitate new production volumes as they are brought online and connect producers to end-users.
- a market in which interstate pipeline development is relatively seamless due to a well-established governing body (i.e. - the Federal Energy Regulatory Commission) and a comparatively straightforward regulatory approval process.
- a market in which demand pull is sufficient, and can materialize with minimal regulatory impediment, to provide the opportunity for new supplies to compete for market share in the energy complex.
- a market where a well-developed service sector already exists that can facilitate fast-paced drilling activity and provide rapid response to demands in the field.
- a service sector that must compete by reducing costs and improving technologies in order to gain a competitive advantage.
- a sizeable rig fleet that is capable of responding to upstream demands without constraint.
- a deep set of upstream actors that includes independent producers that can behave as the "entrepreneur" in the upstream thereby facilitating a flow of capital into the field toward smaller scale, riskier ventures than those typically engaged by vertically integrated majors.

Every one of the above bullets has some relevance to infrastructure – from permitting to access to market function to price formation to investment, etc. If any of these features is absent, an effective barrier to market development is presented, usually manifesting in the form of higher costs. Moreover, some of the above *sufficient* conditions can be co-dependent on the others, which highlights to the notion that well-designed market institutions and regulatory frameworks can be self-reinforcing. For example, a well-developed service sector relies on a deep set of entrepreneurial, independent upstream players to create large demands for its products and

---

[1] For more, see "The Land of Opportunity? Policy, Constraints and Energy Security in North America" by Kenneth B Medlock III, https://www.bakerinstitute.org/research/land-opportunity-policy-constraints-and-energy-security-north-america/.

services, just as the population of independent producers in the US upstream might not be so deep absent a well-developed service sector.

**Figure 1 – Shale Resources in North America**

Source: http://alfin2300.blogspot.com/2012/03/gallery-of-world-hydrocarbon-endowment.html

The coexistence of these factors makes the US a unique environment for upstream shale-directed investments. The result is self-evident, as US oil and gas production have each increased significantly in last decade, driven entirely by shale-directed developments (see Figure 2).

**Figure 2 – US Oil and Gas Production, 2000-2017**

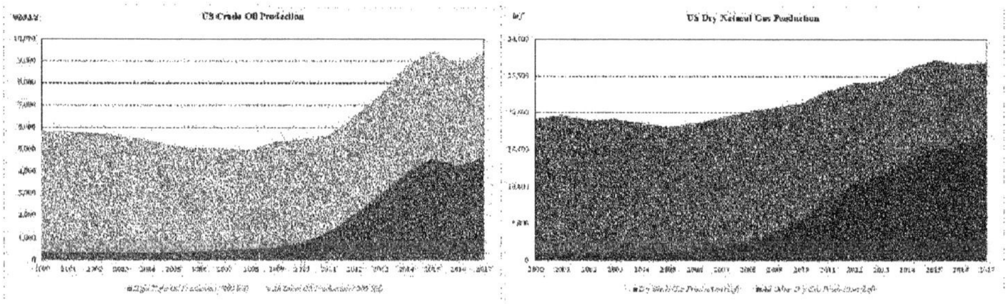

Source: US Energy Information Administration

Concomitant with the growth in US oil and gas production, we have seen significant shifts in the US balance of trade in crude oil, natural gas and petroleum products, with the US now a net exporter of the latter two (see Figure 3). While the US is still a net importer of crude oil, US exports of light crudes have increased substantially since the lifting of the oil export ban, eclipsing 2.5 million barrels per day during the second week of May. This has, in turn, afforded a more efficient, increasingly export-oriented use of US refining infrastructure, which is better suited to handle heavier imported crudes. Weekly data from the US Energy Information Administration indicate that the combined total exports of crude oil and refined products eclipsed 8.3 million barrels per day in late April, up from just under 1.0 million barrels per day in early 2006. This translates into a significant shift in the net balance of trade for US crude oil and petroleum products. Natural gas exports (pipeline and LNG) have also ramped up as new export licenses have been granted with expanding opportunities for profitable export, and the US is now a net exporter of natural gas. Altogether, the expansion of US exports of crude oil, refined products and natural gas have transformed the US from a significant consuming nation that was beholden to policies aimed at securing supplies from foreign countries. Today, the US is a producing nation that can use its energy abundance to wield influence through foreign policy.[2]

**Figure 3 – Net Exports of Natural Gas, Oil and Petroleum Products, Jan 2000-Feb 2018**

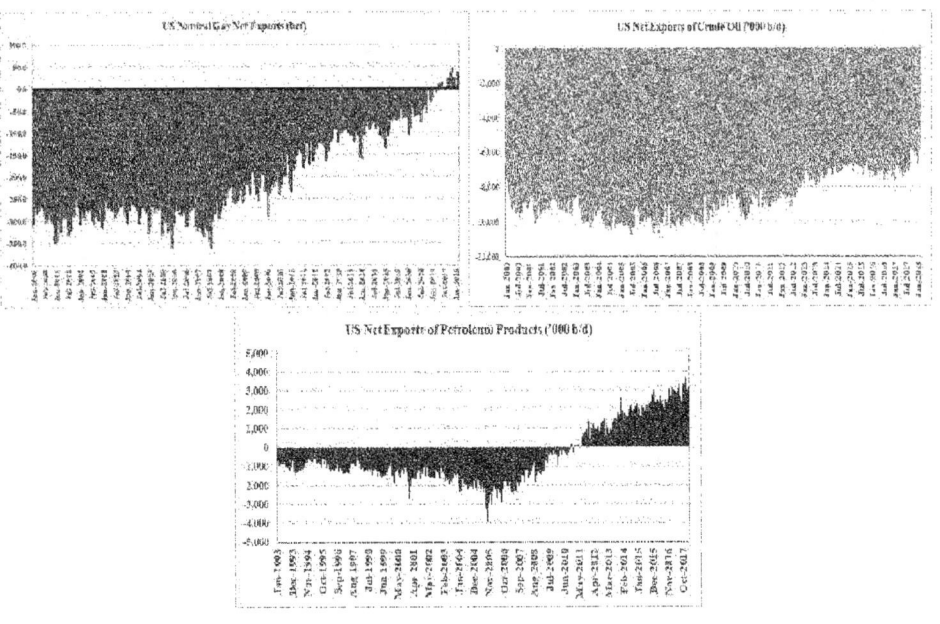

Source: US Energy Information Administration

---

[2] "Geopolitical dimensions of US oil security," Jim Krane and Kenneth B Medlock III, *Energy Policy* (Mar 2018)

Despite this, it is important to recognize that growth in US oil production does not render the US "independent" from other actors in the global oil market. In fact, any disruption of supply from a significant oil exporting nation would trigger an increase in global prices that could be economically and politically destabilizing for importing countries. Oil is an openly traded commodity in a globally fungible market. As such, prices are formed by supply and demand fundamentals, with short-run price movements influenced by factors such as OPEC spare production capacity, rates of global demand growth, inventory levels, geopolitical events, natural disasters and financial markets. Given the global interconnectedness of oil consumers and producers, there is no such thing as *independence* from international oil market perturbations. Even if the United States were to become a net oil exporter, US oil and petroleum product prices would remain exposed to international influences.

Nevertheless, the growth in US oil and gas production is transforming the status quo and shifting the geopolitical balance. This highlights the importance of the so-called "shale revolution" in achieving US geopolitical and foreign policy aims. The legacy of US regulatory and market institutions engenders significant global influence, and today there is much discussion about the US being an "energy superpower." In fact, this terminology has permeated the US State Department and been a recognized facet of diplomacy carried forth by the Bureau of Energy Resources for the past several years, spanning Administrations. Currently, we can see this directly from the Bureau of Energy Resources website.

> ENR promotes U.S. interests globally on critical issues such as: ensuring economic and energy security for the U.S. and our allies and partners; removing barriers to energy development and trade; and promoting U.S. best practices regarding transparency and good governance. In addition, we review applications for the construction, connection, operation, or maintenance of facilities for the exportation or importation of petroleum, petroleum products, coal, and other fuels (except for natural gas) at the borders of the United States.
>
> The Bureau serves as the principal advisor to the Secretary of State on energy security, policy, operations, and programs. Through diplomacy and a wide range of programs, ENR works to ensure worldwide energy security by fostering diverse global energy supplies from all sources of energy.
>
> ENR operates at the critical intersection between energy and U.S. national security, and ensures U.S. leadership on global energy issues. U.S. national security is threatened when:
>
> - Our allies lack reliable access to affordable energy or a diversity of choices;
> - Foreign energy markets shut out U.S. companies;
> - Poor governance prevents market-based energy solutions;
> - Competition for energy leads to conflict; or
> - Terrorists and rogue regimes seek to exploit energy resources to fund violence and destabilizing activities.
>
> To address these challenges, ENR works with leaders at the highest levels of government, business, and civil society, playing a crucial role in achieving U.S. foreign policy objectives in the energy arena. ENR foreign assistance programs are integral to the Bureau's diplomatic engagement overseas and provide critical support for the Department's objectives and the Administration's global diplomacy priorities.
>
> See: https://www.state.gov/e/enr/, accessed Feb 5, 2018

Increasing US oil and gas exports have facilitated the goals set forth by the US State Department. So, the energy renaissance has had direct bearing on US diplomacy. However, the US government is neither the owner nor the producer of mineral wealth in the US, as is the case with government ownership of mineral wealth in many other nations. Thus, the soft power afforded to the US government is facilitated by the unique regulatory and market institutions established in the US that allows the private sector's commercial development of oil and gas.

In general, legal institutions that place mineral rights in the hands of landowners and allow intellectual and physical property to be monetized have led to a regulatory framework in the US that is highly conducive to innovation and entrepreneurial activity across the energy sector. In the oil and gas space, incentives for domestic development derive from transparent, market-driven prices and a low cost to lift and move supplies. Hence, domestic production is very sensitive to the availability of capital and infrastructure. If anything disrupts the availability of either capital or infrastructure, production can grind to a halt in the affected region. This complicates the calculus around policy formation at the federal level, particularly when compared to the local level.[3] In short, domestic policy must continue to support domestic production if foreign policy goals that are facilitated by domestic oil and gas production are to be realized.

As the US increases its exports of crude oil, petroleum products and natural gas, its influence expands into those nations that increasingly rely on imports to satisfy their energy appetites associated with economic growth. In general, expanded US production renders global supply to be more price responsive, and, as a result, carries an energy security benefit to consumers at home and abroad. As argued in previous Baker Institute research, this also benefits US foreign policy endeavors in dealing with potentially hostile oil-producing nations, and provides a stabilizing effect on the global oil market.[4]

*Geopolitics, Energy Security, and Oil and Gas Trade*

There are multiple definitions of the term "geopolitics", but it generally refers to the impact of geography on the balance of power in international affairs. Such geographical elements include things such as access to open seas, topography of countries/regions, and local climate because they each convey information about potential for force projection, national defense capability, and economic prowess. Hence, for the last roughly 100 years, the term has been used to discuss how things such as the industrial revolution as well as technological innovations in transportation and communications would reshape the international political landscape. Over the last few decades, the term has become increasingly used when referring to discussions centered on access to adequate energy supplies and how various international actors could shape international energy

---

[3] See "The Market Impact of New Natural Gas-Directed Policies in the United States" (Feb 2015) by Kenneth Medlock and Peter Hartley, available online at https://www.bakerinstitute.org/research/north-american-energy/.
[4] See "To Lift or Not to Lift? The US Crude Oil Export Ban: Implications for Price and Energy Security" (March 2015) by Kenneth Medlock, available online at https://www.bakerinstitute.org/research/north-american-energy/

trade for political gain. Hence, the concept of energy security has been embroiled in broader discourse concerning geopolitics.

The concept of energy security gained prominence in public policy discourse following the oil price shocks of the 1970s as a negative correlation between oil price and macroeconomic performance in oil-importing countries became increasingly recognized. In this context, "energy security" generally refers to the concept of ensuring an adequate supply of energy at a stable and reasonable price to avoid economic malaise. So, energy security can be captured by three basic concepts: (1) adequacy of supply, (2) stability of price, and (3) relatively low price. First, adequacy of supply follows from the fact that energy is required for virtually all modern economic activity. Second, price stability is important because irregular price volatility can be a source of uncertainty, which (if it negatively impacts investment) carries a negative macroeconomic impact. Third, price level matters because it has a direct impact on household disposable income and industrial/commercial operating budgets; quite simply, if more financial resources are diverted to energy purchases, less is available for other activities. Hence, the concepts of energy security and economic security are intimately linked, as the former, if achieved, facilitates elements of the latter.

Each of these has relevance to the role of the US in the broader geopolitical context, and, of course, domestic energy security and economic well-being. Diversification of the overall energy supply portfolio is one means of ensuring stability in supply at a reasonable price. The ability to access a variety of supply sources is a crucial component in most energy security arguments. For example, the negative impacts of any temporary disruption in supply can be more easily overcome if there is an easily accessible alternative source of supply for the same fuel. It follows, therefore, that diversification of supply is generally viewed to be beneficial for energy security. Europe, for example, has become all too familiar with this over the past decade, as tensions revolving around natural gas payments from Ukraine to Russia have resulted in multiple temporary pressure reductions on pipelines providing supply to Europe from Russia traversing Ukraine.[5] In fact, these disruptions have sparked significant effort to diversify sources of supply across the European Union away from Russia.

This is where the US has an important and growing role to play. In particular, as domestic oil and gas production increases, the US will have a greater impact on global market balance, both by direct export and by displacement. This, in turn, raises an important point about market fungibility. Energy security is facilitated by increasing both spatial and intertemporal trading opportunity in energy commodity markets. In this regard, the US has a distinct economic and geopolitical advantage. As expounded in previous testimony given before the Senate Energy and Natural Resources (SENR) Committee, the existence of infrastructure that allows trade to occur enhances market function thereby providing elements of reliability and security of supply for consumers,

---

[5] "Could trade help achieve energy security?" by Kenneth B Medlock III, World Economic Forum (Mar 3, 2016).

and the regulatory and legal frameworks in the US have historically been conducive to infrastructure investment, especially when compared to other regions around the world[6]

Physical infrastructure enhances market fungibility by connecting markets spatially (via regional trade) and through time (via storage). As a case in point, constraints on the ability to meet the unexpected demand shock in the wake of the disaster at Fukushima in early 2011 resulted in the spot price of Asian LNG rising to unprecedented levels. If LNG export capacity had existed in the US at that time, price increases in Asia would not have been so extreme. This point was not lost on LNG developers as they rushed to acquire permits to export US natural gas as LNG in the years that followed, and the enduring increase in natural gas produced from shale continues to provide ample commercial opportunity to profitably export LNG from the US.

As US LNG exports rise, the global market will become physically linked to North America, the most liquid natural gas market on the world. This should, in turn, facilitate more trade and alter the liquidity paradigm that has characterized the global LNG market heretofore. This emerging reality has triggered enormous interest by consumers in Asia, Europe and Latin America as US-sourced LNG exports are understood to be market-driven and, thus, relatively secure. On the geopolitical front, this means US LNG serves as a "credible threat" to the status quo enjoyed by incumbent regional suppliers – for instance, Russia into Europe or Bolivia into Brazil. Moreover, as the introduction of US LNG enhances market liquidity, it will fundamentally alter the nature of natural gas pricing everywhere.

We have already seen evidence of US LNG as a paradigm altering credible threat in the Baltic region. Upon the opening of the LNG import facility in Lithuania, Russia renegotiated the price on its gas sales to the region in order to maintain its market position. This, of course, means the region still imports Russian natural gas. But, the cost of doing so is now lower and there exists capability to at least partially switch suppliers should Russia use natural gas to exercise any hegemonic intent. Hence, the credible threat of US LNG supply has fundamentally altered the status quo in the Baltic region.[7]

Oil markets are also being fundamentally altered by significant growth in US oil production. As indicated in Figure 4, global oil production has increased by over 18.7 million barrels per day since 1998, and OPEC's market share has held relatively steady over that same period at around 42%. Since 2007, despite OPEC's ability to hold market share, the global oil market has undergone a significant shift as strong growth in US oil production – rising by over 5.4 million barrels per day – has seen the US share of global output rise from 8.3% to 13.4%, representing growth in volume

---

[6] See testimony at SENR full committee hearing on energy infrastructure (Feb 8, 2018). Oral and written testimony as well as questions for the record are available at https://www.energy.senate.gov/public/index.cfm/2018/2/full-committee-hearing-on-energy-infrastructure.

[7] See, "A 'Credible Threat' Approach to Long Run Deterrence of Russian-European Hegemony" by Kenneth B Medlock III available at http://www.forbes.com/sites/thebakersinstitute/2014/03/10/a-credible-threat-approach-to-long-run-deterrence-of-russian-european-hegemony/.

and market share not seen since Saudi Arabian oil production increased by 6.4 million barrels per day over the decade of the 1970s. Notably, the growth in US production has largely offset declines witnessed in other non-OPEC regions, except Russia where output share has also remained stable since 2007.

**Figure 4 – Shares of Global Oil Production by Select Region, Select Years**

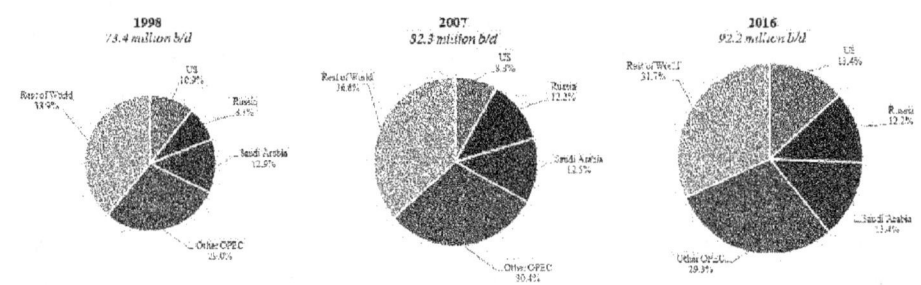

Source: BP Statistical Review

**Figure 5 – Change in Global Oil Production by Country/Region, 2007-2016**

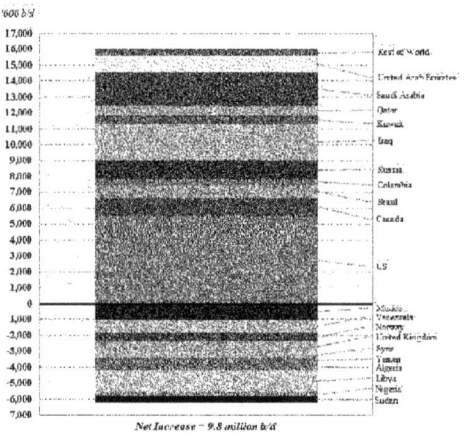

Source: BP Statistical Review

Digging a little deeper in the trends witnessed since 2007 highlights how important US oil production has been for global market balance. As seen in Figure 5, production increased in several countries – such as Saudi Arabia, Iraq, Russia, Brazil, Canada and the US, to name a few – while it decreased in others – such as Mexico, Venezuela, the United Kingdom, and Libya, among others. Among the countries depicted in Figure 4 where production decreased from 2007 through 2016,

Mexico, Venezuela, Syria, Yemen, Algeria, Libya, Nigeria and Sudan all were negatively impacted by various above-ground issues, such as sector mismanagement and domestic civil strife. In sum, this amounted to a decrease of about 5 million barrels per day of supply. The production increase from the US during this same period was about 5.5 million barrels per day, meaning US light tight oil production (shale) accounted for an important source of supply to offset production declines driven by above-ground factors. Moreover, given the declines in the UK and Norway (about 1.2 million barrels per day) and the rapid demand growth seen in developing, non-OECD countries (see Figure 6), US production has provided an incredibly important incremental source of supply.

**Figure 6 – Change in Global Oil Consumption by Country/Region, 2007-2016**

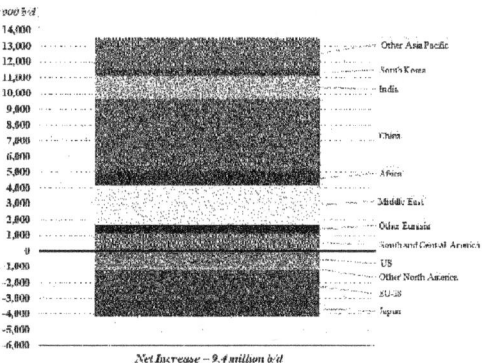

Source: BP Statistical Review

Given the dramatic *net* growth in demand of almost 10 million barrels per day since 2007, driven entirely by the developing world, additional sources of oil supply have been paramount for market balance and broader energy security. Given that US oil production is commercially motivated (rather than dictated by government or national oil company policy), the incremental supplies of US oil to the global market are arguably more secure than supply from virtually anywhere else in the world. As argued in previous research, distinct energy security benefits accrue as more stable and secure sources of crude oil enter the growing global market. Greater stability, in turn, lessens international market oil price volatility, which matriculates through to petroleum product prices. As noted above, it is well-documented that higher prices and greater price volatility are associated with macroeconomic malaise. So, the US has a distinct opportunity to lead an oil industry transformation that could see lines of global oil trade redrawn as North American production captures a larger portion of the growing international market. This will, if fully realized, have tremendous implications for US foreign policy endeavors in its dealings with countries such as Iran, Venezuela and Russia. For example, to the extent that US oil production is price responsive, the US government can act with greater impunity in using targeted sanctions to dissuade hegemonic behavior. In addition, US oil supply will lend greater stability to the global crude oil market thereby conveying benefits to the US and its allies.

*Concluding remarks*

Energy is critical to modern economic activity. This is, in fact, why energy security concerns – either discussed in the context of domestic reliability or international access – are such an important component of energy policy discourse. Just 15 years ago, the consensus view was that US oil and gas production would be in inexorable decline, and the US would be a growing *importer* of both fuels. However, upstream innovations have shifted the competitive landscape in global oil and natural gas markets, to the point where now the US is a growing *supplier* of oil and gas to global markets. This has been propelled by a robust, technically and commercially recoverable resource endowment in the US and the unique set of regulatory and market institutions that have promoted commercial development of infrastructure; each has conveyed significant benefit in the energy security domain and will carry a significant $21^{st}$ century competitive advantage to US interests. This becomes even more salient when one considers the anticipated growth of emerging markets in developing Asia over the next 20 to 30 years. The sheer collective size of these markets – over 3 billion people in economies projected to grow in excess of 5% per year – will put steady pressure on supply lines for all fuels, meaning the US with its relative abundance of oil and gas is well-positioned to play an important role in shaping energy geopolitics for the next few decades.

Mr. POE. Thank you, Mr. Medlock.
Mr. Carroll.

## STATEMENT OF MR. DAVID CARROLL, PRESIDENT AND CHIEF EXECUTIVE OFFICER, GAS TECHNOLOGY INSTITUTE

Mr. CARROLL. Thank you.

Chairman Poe, Ranking Member, Keating, members of the subcommittee, thanks for the opportunity to provide some testimony today.

David Carroll, president of the Gas Technology Institute—a Chicago-based independent not-for-profit research organization that turns raw technology into meaningful high-impact energy solutions that benefit both the economy and the environment.

And I have the current additional honor of serving as the president of the International Gas Union. My term wraps up next month as the U.S. prepares to host the World Gas Conference right here in Washington.

As my colleague, Dr. Medlock, just indicated, while shale gas might seem like an overnight success to many, decades of research by GTI, the U.S. Department of Energy, and industry really provided the technical understanding needed to produce this abundant resource.

And when GTI and Mitchell Energy back in 1991 completed the first horizontal well in the Barnett, the U.S. energy transformation had begun.

So you fast forward to today, and oil and gas production from U.S. shale has become the world's swing supply, arguably the biggest energy breakthrough in the last 50 years.

The oil and gas sector generates $1.2 trillion in GDP and over 9 million U.S. jobs. But a powerful impact of shale gas is the reduced prices to everyday consumers and families.

Increased use of gas in electricity generation has reduced $CO_2$ emissions from the power sector by 27 percent. U.S. net energy imports have decreased from 30 percent of our total energy needs in 2005 to about 7 percent last year.

And with the expansion of domestic energy production from multiple sources including renewables in steady strides in energy efficiency, we are approaching energy independence.

Shale gas has also enabled greater participation in the global gas market. Let me give you a few stats from IGU's 2018 world LNG report, which is issuing next month.

Global trade in LNG last year grew by 10 percent, or 35 million tons, as projects in Australia and the United States came online.

China alone represented one-half of the global growth in LNG last year, as it shifts its energy mix toward natural gas and away from coal in its effort to fight air pollution.

Qatar remains the world's largest LNG exporter with about 30 percent of the global market. Australia was second. The U.S. was sixth.

There were over 90 million tons of liquefaction capacity that are under construction right now, but a third of that comes onstream this year in six countries, including Australia, the U.S., and Russia.

So U.S. LNG now competes in a dynamic market with an increasing number of producers and consumers, and yes, we are now a major exporter.

But our success is not assured. Our competitors are not standing still. They're investing. They're expanding. So we must make efforts to enhance productivity in upstream production and expand transportation networks and liquefaction processes to keep pace.

A few comments about demand—about 70 percent of global demand in liquefied natural gas will occur in non-OECD countries. Let's take India, for example, which has an ambitious goal of increasing gas in its energy mix from 6 percent today to 15 percent over the next 15 years.

LNG imports are going to play a role, as will more domestic production, nationwide pipeline construction, and new city gas distribution networks. Helping India enhance its energy security, promoting its economic development, and improving the environment is in our interests as a country.

Last June, President Trump and Prime Minister Modi announced the U.S.-India Strategic Energy Partnership, affirming the importance of our bilateral relationship.

Secretary Perry recently travelled to New Delhi where he and Energy Minister Pradhan co-chaired the inaugural meeting of this partnership.

As GTI's CEO, I've been in India over three times in the last 18 months and have executed MOUs with two institutions to train India's expanding energy workforce.

So these are, indeed, exciting times for natural gas in India, to use them as an example, now the world's fourth largest importer of LNG.

So, in conclusion, innovation in the natural gas sector affords opportunities to enhance our economy, create jobs, save consumers money, and engage in global trade. It's bolstered by—it has bolstered our energy security and really given us the flexibility in dealing with strategic partners around the world.

It's important to remember that this success didn't happen overnight, and it didn't happen by accident. So sustaining our progress will require continued investments in research and infrastructure.

Thank you for the opportunity to testify, and I look forward to your questions.

[The prepared statement of Mr. Carroll follows:]

**gti.**

Testimony of
David C. Carroll
President and Chief Executive Officer
Gas Technology Institute

Before the
Committee on Foreign Affairs
Subcommittee on Terrorism, Nonproliferation and Trade
U.S. House of Representatives

May 22, 2018

"Geopolitics of U.S. Oil and Gas Competitiveness"

*Preface: Gas Technology Institute (GTI) is an independent 501(c)(3) research organization, established as an Illinois not-for-profit corporation. GTI has a 75-year history that stems from two predecessor organizations—the Institute of Gas Technology (IGT) established in 1941 as an education and research performing organization, and Gas Research Institute (GRI), created in 1976 to manage a cooperative research and development (R&D) program on natural gas. Based on a settlement between FERC and the gas industry in 1998, the traditional GRI RD&D program—and the mandatory funding to support it—ended in 2004. Today GTI is a voluntarily funded organization developing technology-based solutions for consumers, industry, and government.*

Chairman Poe, Ranking Member Keating, and Members of the Subcommittee, on behalf the employees of the Gas Technology Institute (GTI), I thank you for this opportunity to testify before you today regarding U.S. Oil and Gas Competitiveness and the Geopolitical Implications.

My name is David Carroll, President and Chief Executive Officer at GTI. I oversee GTI's entire staff and operations, which focus on enhancing unconventional gas supply, energy conversion, natural gas delivery, and improved efficiency in end use markets. Prior to joining GTI in 2001, I held various technical and commercial positions in the global chemical industry with Air Products and Chemicals, Inc. and Praxair, Inc.

GTI is a leading non-profit research, development, and training organization, and our mission is to turn raw technology into practical energy solutions that have meaningful impacts on the economy and the environment. We celebrated our 75th anniversary as an institute in 2016 and have spent the last seven decades creating innovative solutions to critical challenges along the entire gas value chain, improving the ways of producing, transporting, converting and using energy to benefit the general public.

We cover a robust spectrum of initiatives. In addition to reducing the environmental footprint of shale gas production, which you'll hear more about, GTI's focus includes:

- Expanding the supply of natural gas and renewable energy
- Developing cleaner and renewable alternatives to petroleum-based transportation fuels and chemicals
- Enhancing the integrity of our nation's vast pipeline infrastructure
- Reducing methane emissions across the value chain
- Promoting energy efficiency by developing and demonstrating high-efficiency technologies
- Advancing clean, low-cost power production from all of our energy resources

With more than 360 employees across the nation, GTI engineers and scientists are developing innovative new tools, technologies, and methodologies, and delivering science-based factual data that helps guide informed decision-making and enlightened policy development.

GTI and its predecessor organizations, the Institute of Gas Technology (IGT) and the Gas Research Institute (GRI) have a storied history rich in meaningful Public-Private Partnerships on various energy related topics, especially in the development of our country's unconventional oil and gas resources.

I currently have the additional honor of serving as President of the International Gas Union or IGU. This global association spans 91 countries, representing 97% of the world's production and use of natural gas. IGU is a non-profit based in Barcelona, Spain, and its member associations and companies are dedicated to enhancing the operational, technical and economic performance of the global gas industry and improving the quality of life for our fellow citizens through natural gas. The American Gas Association is the U.S. charter member of the IGU as are its global counterparts.

IGU is the owner of the World Gas Conference, a massive triennial event that takes place next month at the Walter E. Washington Convention Center right here in Washington. This conference and exhibition has not been held in the U.S. since 1988, so I hope that you will have the opportunity to join thousands of energy professionals, government leaders and policy makers from around the world.

**U.S. Shale Development: Revolution or Evolution?**

While shale development seems like an overnight occurrence to most, decades of research underpin the technical understanding and complexities of producing this almost seemingly impermeable resource. GRI and DOE conducted a focused research program addressing fracturing and production of shale formations during the 1980s and 1990s, investing more than $100 million.

Much of what now is considered seminal research was conducted in a series of field experiments that took place in eastern U.S. shales. Researchers from industry, national labs, and universities studied the data sets from empirical field tests of these wells and successfully built important fracture models and other innovations that have accelerated shale production over time. It is of interest to note that this research was criticized by much of industry at the time, with some large exploration and production companies describing the research as a "waste of money". Two men, former GRI President Dr. Henry Linden and George Mitchell, CEO of Mitchell Energy who served on the GRI Board of Directors at that time, fortunately did not share this sentiment.

Mitchell expressed support for shale research, but recommended moving the research program to new geologic basins. In 1991 GRI worked with Mitchell Energy to drill the Stella Young well in the Barnett Shale in Texas — a horizontal well stimulated with new technology that produced three times more gas than any other well up to that time. This was a pivotal point in the U.S. shale gas evolution that transformed the energy industry.

**Impact of Upstream Development - Shale by the Numbers:**

In addition to the research and technology underpinning that occurred over decades, the U.S. has a unique alignment of factors that no other country in the world enjoys that has made shale development such an astounding success:

- Incredible, vast resource of brittle shale
- Mineral rights ownership by landowners

- Great access to capital
- Tremendous pipeline infrastructure
- Robust service sector
- Entrepreneurial spirit of the independent producer
- Public policy that provides incentives for development

Fast forward to today, oil and gas production from U.S. shale formations has become what most consider the world's "swing supply", a truly amazing success and likely the biggest energy breakthrough of the last 50 years. While the oil and gas sector is responsible for an estimated $1.2 trillion in GDP and 9.3 million U.S. jobs, one of the most meaningful and visible impacts of shale gas is lower utility bills for consumers, putting $1,372 back into the pockets of the average American family, according to a Perryman Group study. Since shale gas is used to heat homes and produce electricity, consumers are seeing the impacts in both natural gas and electricity bills. The increased use of natural gas in electricity generation has also produced significant reductions in $CO_2$ from the power sector – 27.8% from 2005 to 2017, according to EIA.

Net energy imports have decreased from 30 Quadrillion Btus (Quads) in 2005 – over 30% of our total energy needs in that year – to only 7.4 Quads in 2017 and just 7.6% of our domestic energy needs. With continued expansion of domestic energy production from multiple sources – natural gas, oil, biomass, wind, and solar – and steady strides in energy efficiency, we are heading closer to full net energy independence.

**Liquefied Natural Gas - Imports to Exports**

In addition to the myriad benefits to the U.S. economy, shale gas has given our country the opportunity to participate more broadly in the global gas trade, both through pipeline gas to Mexico and through exports of liquefied natural gas, or LNG, to more distant markets.

At next month's World Gas Conference, IGU will release the latest edition of its much anticipated World LNG Report, which highlights recent trends and statistics in the global LNG market. I've provided below some excerpts from this report to give you a sense of the vibrancy of this global market in which the U.S. now vigorously competes.

"International trade in liquefied natural gas (LNG) continues to be one of the most vibrant segments of the world's natural gas value chain, growing in 2017 by 35.2 million tonnes (MT), or 45.8 billion cubic meters, of natural gas, to 293.1 MT in global trade. That represents growth of over 10% and comes as projects in Australia and the U.S. bring new capacity on line and Asian markets continue to grow. China and South Korea led Asian growth with additional demand of 12.7 MT and 4.9 MT, respectively. China has focused on aggregate energy demand toward natural gas and away from coal in its fight against air pollution.

In 2017, more traditional European trade patterns returned, including a move away from LNG re-loading due to overall supply increases and stable demand. Spain, Italy, Portugal and France returned to more traditional LNG uptake. In North America, Mexican imports of LNG were up, as additional low-cost U.S. shale gas imports were unavailable due to pipeline delays. Unlike

2016, the increases in world trade occurred without new major entrants to the world LNG market.

Qatar continued to be the world's leading exporter of LNG, with 2017 liquefaction reaching 81.0 million tonnes per annum (MTPA), followed by Australia, Malaysia, Nigeria, Indonesia, and the U.S. Australia and the U.S. led in growth of exports by increases over 2016 of 11.9 MTPA and 10.2 MTPA, respectively. There are 92 MTPA of liquefaction capacity under construction world-wide, and we expect about one-third to come online this year in far-reaching locations of Australia, Cameroon, Indonesia, Malaysia, Russia, and the United States.

Thus far, the global market is absorbing new supply with minimal distortion, as new buyers and existing markets alike demonstrate a high need for natural gas to meet growing energy demand. The need for cleaner fuels that are available on-demand is a key part of this trend. Non-long-term trade (which includes "spot market" activity) increased yet again, reaching over 88 MT in 2017.

U.S. shale gas continues to moderate North American natural gas prices through technology and efficiency improvements, which translates into lower U.S. feedstock costs. Global LNG prices have seen a rebound as dictated by the international supply/demand balance. Average Northeast Asian spot prices have increased $1.33/MMBtu from 2016 to 2017, and averaged $9.88/MMBtu in January 2018, which is the highest price point in three years. Incremental supply during 2018 will impact the balance and may moderate prices."

As you can see from the above, U.S. LNG is participating in a fast growing, dynamic marketplace with an increasing number of producers and consumers. The U.S. is emerging as a major exporter and will solidify that position as additional liquefaction facilities come on line over the next couple of years.

But our success as an exporter is not assured. It's a competitive market, and the competitors are not standing still, so continued efforts to enhance productivity and reduce costs in our upstream production, transportation network and liquefaction processes will be necessary to keep pace.

U.S. LNG has its advantages, from relatively low cost supply, to flexible contracting and business models, to transparent pricing, to competent reliable producers with access to gas resources and capital. But we have some disadvantages also, not the least of which are higher transportation costs to the growth markets of Asia and Africa. Again, diligent efforts to bring innovation to the LNG value chain will help the U.S. emerge as a leader in this attractive global market.

**India – A Strategic Partner Building a Gas Based Economy**

Now a few words about the global demand for gas. The International Energy Agency (IEA) expects roughly 70% of demand growth over the next twenty years to take place in non OECD countries. We're seeing this today, as developing countries in Asia, Africa and the Middle East look to fuel growing economies, sustain ever growing, urbanizing populations and address the acute problem of poor urban air quality. Natural gas is helping these economies meet these challenges effectively and in a way that doesn't break the bank.

While the examples are many, let me focus on India to illustrate the important role of natural gas. Prime Minister Modi, Energy Minister Pradhan and other authorities have established a goal of increasing the share of gas in their direct energy mix from 6% to 15% over the next 15 years, a massive challenge in a growing economy. LNG will play a role in India's gas supply, as will enhanced domestic production, pipeline infrastructure development and city gas distribution network buildout. Helping India succeed in this initiative, enhancing their energy security, fueling their economic development all the while improving their environment is in the U.S. interests in many ways.

Our government sees this clearly and has responded accordingly. In June of 2017, President Trump and Prime Minister Modi announced the U.S.-India Strategic Energy Partnership (SEP), affirming the strategic importance of our bilateral relationship against the backdrop of one of the most critical and fundamental sectors: energy. Last month, Secretary Perry traveled to New Delhi where he and Petroleum Minister Pradhan co-chaired the inaugural meeting of the US-India Strategic Energy Partnership. SEP has four primary pillars, including one on oil and natural gas, and the goals are simple, yet aspirational: universal energy access, strengthened energy security and increased energy efficiency. The Partnership will create opportunities for advancing favorable policies and commercial sector investment in their emerging gas market. While India's goals and ambitions are bold, they lack much of the necessary infrastructure to bring gas into the country, and to distribute it throughout India. The Partnership should help.

GTI has similarly responded to help India build its capacity to embrace natural gas. As GTI's CEO I've been in India three times over the last 18 months, meeting with government and industry leaders to explore areas of potential cooperation. Earlier this month, GTI signed Memoranda of Understanding to formerly cooperate with two institutions, Pandit Deendayal Petroleum University (PDPU) and LNG importer Petronet LNG, Ltd. Much of our early focus will be to train and develop India's energy workforce, from engineering students, to plant operators and technicians, to mid-career technical and management professionals. Under the Prime Minister Modi's leadership, these are exciting times for natural gas in India.

It's interesting to note that while I was India three weeks ago, a shipment of LNG exited the Cove Point, Maryland LNG facility enroute to Petronet's receiving terminal in Dahej Terminal. India is now the world's fourth largest LNG importer and growing, behind only Japan, China and South Korea. The future is bright for LNG, and natural gas more broadly, in India. The U.S. should continue its efforts to support the development of energy supply, infrastructure, and markets of this important strategic partner.

**How Do We Expand our Competitive Position and Expand our Global Reach**

In the past decade, the U.S. has gone from high oil and gas prices, scarcity and planned import terminals to sustained low prices, 100+ year supplies and an increasing number of export facilities. U.S. shale development has turned the energy landscape upside down.

As we examine the global energy landscape, the U.S. has two things that separate us from everyone else: abundant natural resources and a robust infrastructure. We are fortunate enough to have 2.5 million miles of pipelines that deliver these critical assets across the country. However, the U.S. is not the lowest cost exporting producer of natural gas even with our expansive shale reserves, and only better recovery factors through continued technology advancement can change this paradigm. The most proven path to broadly enhance results in the subsurface is via Public-Private Partnerships, as demonstrated in the following example.

**The Permian Project: GTI's Hydraulic Fracturing Test Site (HFTS):**

*Our goal is simple* – substantially advance the hydraulic fracturing process to optimize well spacing so that fewer wells are needed to effectively improve resource recovery and reduce the environmental footprint of production.

*The problem is multifaceted* – subsurface completion science has the greatest uncertainty and variability of the shale development process. Yet, even as hydraulic fracturing is in wide use, it continues to be a complex and controversial process with many variables that affect the locations at which the fractures propagate, their dimensions, and their ability to enhance production of hydrocarbons. The actual internal architectures of the fractures created along the horizontal holes that are drilled during each stage are not well understood. While we know that the fractures form a complex three-dimensional pattern, direct and reliable data is still needed about the size, shape, and distance of hydraulic fracturing propagation.

Solving this complicated problem requires input from scientific, engineering, and operating subject matter experts from across the industry (operators and service providers), universities, national laboratories, and other research institutes, and the only realistic way to do this is via a Public-Private Partnership. So with the assistance of a cooperative agreement in the amount of $7.4MM from U.S. DOE Fossil Energy, GTI was able to attract:

- A **host site partner** in Laredo Petroleum that provided an eleven horizontal well test bed in the Permian, pertinent micro-seismic and other background data with an approximate value of $100MM, and approximately 25 engineers and operations staff for the experiment.
- A **Joint Industry Partnership** (JIP) of service companies, independent producers, and integrated majors that sponsored the additional $16MM of research work and also provided subject matter experts to technically contribute to the program. (JIP participants are Chevron, ConocoPhillips, Core Laboratories, Devon, Discovery Natural Resources, Encana, Energen, ExxonMobil, Halliburton, Shell, and TOTAL.)
- A team of **leading researchers** at the University of Texas (UT) Petroleum Engineering Department, at the UT Bureau of Economic Geology, and at the National Energy Testing Laboratory.

**The key differentiator of this field experiment is the 600 feet of unique core that was obtained by drilling a one-of-a-kind core well through created hydraulic fractures at the test site.** Extracting core of this magnitude is an expensive and risky undertaking, but all participants agreed in advance that this ground truth evidence is paramount to understanding fractures, validating and developing models, and to consider if and how big data and predictive analytics can improve the process.

The analysis of fracture properties as impacted by reservoir rock conditions will help researchers develop a cause-and-effect relationship between fracturing parameters and reservoir rock to measure the consequences of fracturing—results that can be applied to other locations and plays. Important data about subsurface fracture propagation and proppant transport dynamics will lead to the design of optimal fracture treatments and, ultimately, ideal well spacing. Many of the findings will likely be transferrable to other basins, but shale is a heterogeneous resource so much more work needs to be done.

**Conclusion:**

In conclusion, innovation in the natural gas sector over the last couple of decades has given our nation tremendous opportunities to enhance the competitiveness of our economy, create jobs, save consumers money and engage more broadly in global trade. Developing this abundant domestic resource has enhanced our nation's energy security and provided more flexibility in dealing with strategic partners around the world.

It's important to remember that this success in natural gas didn't happen overnight and it didn't happen by accident. And sustaining our progress will require continued investments in research to enhance well productivity, reduce costs and minimize the overall environmental impacts of production, transportation and use. We also need continued investments in pipeline infrastructure to get this affordable, cleaner energy to market.

There are many stakeholders in the natural gas space: employees, customers, consumers, investors, national and local governments, regulators, environmental groups and others. Our industry is working hard to constructively engage these stakeholder groups to stress the benefits from gas that accrue to our broader economy. Reinforcement of these benefits by our national leaders and policy makers to stakeholders of all demographics would help ensure that we realize the full economic, strategic and environmental benefits of natural gas for decades to come.

Thank you for the opportunity to provide this testimony.

David C. Carroll
President and CEO, GTI

Mr. POE. Thank you, Mr. Carroll.
Ms. Ladislaw.

**STATEMENT OF MS. SARAH LADISLAW, DIRECTOR AND SENIOR FELLOW, ENERGY AND NATIONAL SECURITY PROGRAM, CENTER FOR STRATEGIC AND INTERNATIONAL STUDIES**

Ms. LADISLAW. Thank you.

Good afternoon, Chairman Poe, Ranking Member Keating, and members of the subcommittee. It's my pleasure to be here and to talk with you today about the geopolitics of U.S. oil and gas competitiveness.

My remarks and testimony represent my views and not my colleagues and my institution.

As has been stated, the United States has experienced an oil and natural gas production renaissance that has changed the domestic and global energy landscape in some really important ways.

The most direct linkage between U.S. oil and gas competitiveness and geopolitics is the contribution it makes to global and U.S. energy security.

First, it provides additional supply to a previously tight market; second, U.S. tight oil adds a new kind of supply to the market that takes months rather than years to ramp up and can serve as a relief valve when markets are tight; third, the new oil and gas supply source has added a sense of resource optimism to the market.

Today, producers, consumers, and investors understand that given the right price environment and investment conditions, new oil and gas supplies can be brought to market.

The U.S. oil and natural gas supply surge is also good for the U.S. economy and national security, as has also been mentioned.

Oil and gas production in the United States is an important source of job creation, economic growth, has provided crucial stimulus to the economy during the post-Great Recession period, and improves our balance of trade.

The benefits of U.S. oil and gas competitiveness should not, however, obscure the risks that still exist to U.S. energy security. Despite the rising level of exports, the United States still imports a good deal of oil and natural gas.

As we approach a new hurricane season, it's important not to forget the oil, gas, and electricity supply disruptions that resulted from Hurricanes Harvey and Irma in 2017.

Finally, even the abundant supply of domestic oil and natural gas is not a direct proxy for security. Delivery systems are needed to get resources from the point of production to the point of consumption, and in many cases, we experience bottlenecks in that part of the energy system.

The U.S. oil and gas supply renaissance is also a good news story for the places where energy intersects with geopolitics.

First, as I noted in my June 27 testimony to the House Foreign Affairs Subcommittee on the Western Hemisphere, North America is now one of the most energy-advantaged regions in the whole planet.

The energy resources contained in Canada, Mexico, and the United States are second to none, and when combined with the region's stable legal system, liberalized trading environment, cross-border infrastructure, high-tech industries, and educated and competitive labor force, it's hard to match in terms of its potential.

It's important to look at the U.S. relationship with Canada and Mexico as an opportunity to build on these natural advantages.

Second, U.S. oil and gas can add to the diversity of supply available to other countries in helpful ways. One key example is the additional supplies made available to Europe.

The availability of additional supply sources was part of the equation that led to the capture of—excuse me, the departure of oil index pricing and long-term gas contracts in Europe.

As my colleague at CSIS has recently written, this does not mean Europe is less dependent on Russia for its gas supplies necessarily. In 2017, Europe actually increased gas imports from Russia, along with other countries.

The additional import options and availability of global supplies are, of course, good for Europe's gas supply security, but, has not in reality lessened the energy ties between Europe and Russia, nor has it fundamentally changed the geopolitical dynamics within the region with regard to Ukraine.

Third, major oil-producing economies like Saudi Arabia, Russia, and other members of the Organization of Petroleum Exporting Countries, or OPEC, have had to reevaluate a number of oil market and geopolitical factors as it relates to U.S. tight oil production.

First, the oil price drop in 2014 that resulted from a variety of factors, including the rapid onset of U.S. oil supply growth and subsequent period of low prices caused OPEC to reevaluate its position within the market, both in 2014 and again in 2016.

In order to be effective, Saudi Arabia, as the leader of OPEC, struck up an alliance with Russia and several other non-OPEC countries to withhold oil supply from the market in order to stabilize prices until markets came to rebalance.

It's unclear how deep and abiding the alliance between Russia and Saudi Arabia is beyond their current market management arrangement.

But the relationship has been accompanied by a deepening of Russian diplomatic and investment activity throughout the Middle East.

The second effect on major supplying countries is the area of economic planning and diversification. The most notable example of this is the economic and social reform plan launched in 2016 called Saudi Vision 2030.

Through this plan, Saudi Arabia intends to revamp its domestic economy to rely less on oil and diversify its income sources.

Leaving the challenges of implementing this vision aside, it's important to note that many countries that depend on oil-derived revenue to fund their governments have taken steps to insulate their economies from periods of sustained low prices.

This, of course, has been done in the face of low oil prices. So the sustainability of those reforms may be in question when prices rise again, but the reforms were a direct result of the oil price drop brought on by U.S. supply.

Notably, countries like Venezuela, once among the largest and most successful oil-producing countries in the world, have suffered a great deal under the pressure of low oil prices after years of neglect and mismanagement under the current and previous leadership.

One often hears it asserted that the increased production of U.S. oil and gas has served to lessen U.S. reliance or entanglement in the Middle East. In fact, this has hardly been the case.

The perceived U.S. withdrawal from the Middle East was sparked by a desire to draw down in the wartime posture of the Middle East and shift the strategic focus to striking a security balance in Asia.

The U.S. is no freer from entanglements in the Middle East than it was before the onset of U.S. oil and gas supply revolution, though it is less concerned about energy security thanks to the low oil price environment of the last several years.

Following the release and announcement of the U.S. intention to withdraw from the Joint Comprehensive Plan of Action—the Iran agreement—the Trump administration showed that the U.S. still relies on Middle East oil supplies to help guarantee price stability in the region.

As I have written in other publications, energy and foreign policy are often inextricably intertwined. But the ability for policymakers to use very—to use energy resources as tools of targeted foreign policy leverage or even energy dominance is misguided.

I will be happy to take any questions.

[The prepared statement of Ms. Ladislaw follows:]

**CSIS** | CENTER FOR STRATEGIC & INTERNATIONAL STUDIES

Statement Before the

House Foreign Affairs

Subcommittee on Terrorism, Nonproliferation, and Trade

## "Geopolitics of U.S. Oil and Gas Competitiveness"

A Testimony by:

### Sarah Ladislaw

Director and Senior Fellow, Energy and National Security Program

Center for Strategic and International Studies

May 22, 2018

2200 Rayburn House Office Building

Good morning Chairman Poe, Ranking Member Keating and members of the subcommittee. It is my pleasure to be here today to speak with you about the *Geopolitics of U.S. Oil and Gas Competitiveness*. My name is Sarah Ladislaw and I direct the Energy and National Security Program at the Center for Strategic and International Studies (CSIS). CSIS is a bipartisan, nonprofit organization headquartered in Washington, D.C. The CSIS Energy and National Security Program provides strategic insights and policy solutions related to the dynamic and changing global energy landscape. My remarks and written testimony represent my views and not the views of my colleagues or CSIS as an institution.

The United States has experienced an oil and natural gas production renaissance that has changed the domestic and global energy landscape in some important ways. Today, U.S. production of oil and natural gas are at or above historical levels. According to the Energy Information Administration (EIA), U.S. crude oil production averaged 10.5 million barrels per day in April 2018 and U.S. natural gas production averaged 85.75 billion cubic feet per day in the same month.[1] Taking into account oil, natural gas, and hydrocarbon gas liquids, the United States is the largest hydrocarbon producer in the world – larger than Russia or Saudi Arabia – and for the last several years the U.S. has been the premier destination for oil and gas investment, attracting billions of dollars in exploration, production and refining of oil, natural gas, and hydrocarbon gas liquids. The United States is exporting more crude oil, oil-derived products, and natural gas than ever before and is poised to be a net exporter of energy by 2022, under certain assumptions. Crude oil exports from the United States averaged over 1 million barrels per day in 2017, while finished product and liquid exports averaged over 5 million barrels per day, and natural gas exports were over 3 trillion cubic feet in 2017.

The most direct linkage between U.S. oil and gas competitiveness and geopolitics is the contribution it makes to global and U.S. energy security. In this regard, U.S. oil and gas production provides some significant benefits and augments global energy security in at least three important ways. First, it provides additional supply to a global market that had been tight for several years as global oil producers raced to keep up with growing Chinese oil demand. In 2008, U.S. crude oil production stood at around 5 million barrels per day compared to the 10.7 million barrels per day average production level expected for 2018, just 10 years later.[2] This is the largest increment of oil production growth ever and its volume is equivalent to the production of the second largest country in OPEC. The addition of almost 6 million barrels per day of crude oil production is a small but important part of the global crude market that today is about 81 million barrels per day.[3] Second, U.S. tight oil adds a new kind of oil supply to the market that takes months, rather than years to ramp up from investment to production. This so-called short cycle oil has the potential to serve as a relief valve when markets are tight, with the ability to bring new supplies to market much more quickly than in years past.

---

[1] Short-Term Energy Outlook, May 8, 2018, Energy Information Administration, https://www.eia.gov/outlooks/steo/
[2] Energy Information Administration, https://www.eia.gov/dnav/pet/pet_crd_crpdn_adc_mbbl_m.htm
[3] Monthly Oil Market Review, May 16, 2018m International Energy Agency.

Third, the new oil and gas supply source has added a sense of resource optimism to the market. Broadly speaking, the advent of tight oil and shale gas development has ushered in an era of perceived resource abundance. Today, producers, consumers, and investors understand that given the right price environment and investment conditions, new oil and gas supplies can and will be brought to market. This is happening at the same time that alternatives to oil and gas are also growing more cost-competitive. The net result has been an energy market that is much more competitive for energy producers with a great deal more variety and options for consumers.

The U.S. oil and natural gas supply surge is also good for the U.S. economy and national security. First, oil and gas production in the United States is an important source of job creation. Oil and gas production has made important contributions to economic growth and provided crucial stimulus to the economy during the post-Great Recession period. As noted earlier, it has encouraged investment in low-cost oil and gas as both a final product and as feedstock for refining and petrochemical ventures. Finally, increasing exports and declining imports of oil and gas has served to improve the U.S. trade balance. On national security grounds, while the United States still faces significant energy vulnerabilities, it is arguably more energy secure today than it was a decade ago because of the oil and gas supply abundance within the U.S. border.

The benefits of U.S. oil and gas competitiveness should not, however, obscure the risks that still exist to U.S. energy security. Despite the rising level of exports, the United States still imports a good deal of oil and natural gas. In fact, the U.S. is more engaged in global oil trade today on a gross basis than ever. This means the U.S. economy continues to experience the impact of oil price changes, just in increasingly complex ways. In addition to price shocks, the United States is still vulnerable to oil and gas supply disruptions. As we approach a new hurricane season it is important not to forget the oil, gas and electricity supply disruptions that resulted from Hurricanes Harvey and Irma in 2017. Hurricane Harvey reduced gross inputs to Gulf Coast refiners by 3.2 million barrels per day, while Hurricane Irma cut power to nearly two thirds of Florida's electricity customers and led to higher gasoline prices. Nearly 22,000 people are still without power in Puerto Rico to this day.

Finally, even the abundant supply of domestic oil and natural gas is not a direct proxy for security – delivery systems are needed to get resources from the point of production to the point of consumption. Logistical bottlenecks in pipeline contracting, sighting, permitting, and construction continues to impede rapidly growing oil and gas production in the Permian Basin in Texas from reaching end markets. While this bottleneck is temporary, it once again illustrates the strategic importance of midstream and delivery infrastructure towards realizing the full commercial and strategic value of these resources.

The U.S. oil and gas supply renaissance is also a good news story for the places where energy intersects with geopolitics. First, as I noted in my June 2017 testimony to the House Foreign

Affairs Subcommittee on the Western Hemisphere, North America is now one of the most energy-advantaged regions on the planet.[4] The energy resources (oil, natural gas, coal, nuclear, wind, solar, and biomass) contained in Canada, Mexico, and the United States are second to none, and when combined with the region's stable legal system, liberalized trading environment, cross-border infrastructure, high-tech industries, and educated and competitive labor force, it is hard to match in terms of potential. It is important to look to the U.S. relationship with Canada and Mexico as an opportunity to build upon these natural advantages.

Second, U.S. oil and gas supply can add to the diversity of supply available to other countries in helpful ways. One key example is the impact of additional gas supplies available to Europe. The availability of additional supply sources was part of the equation that led to a departure of oil-indexed pricing in long-term gas supply contracts in Europe. As my colleague Nikos Tsafos has recently written, this does not mean Europe is less dependent on Russia for its gas supplies.[5] In 2017, Europe actually increased gas imports from Russia along with other countries. The additional import options and availability of global supplies are of course good for Europe's gas supply security but has not in reality lessened the energy ties between Europe and Russia, nor has it fundamentally changed the geopolitical dynamics within the region with regard to Ukraine.

Third, major oil producing countries like Saudi Arabia, Russia, and other members of the Organization of Petroleum Exporting Countries (OPEC) have had to reevaluate a number of oil market and geopolitical factors as it relates to U.S. tight oil production. First, the oil price drop in 2014 that resulted from a variety of factors including the rapid onset of U.S. oil supply growth and subsequent period of low prices, caused OPEC to reevaluate its position within the market both in 2014 and again in 2016. In order to be effective, Saudi Arabia, as the leader of OPEC, struck up an alliance with Russia and several other non-OPEC countries to withhold oil supplies from the market in order to stabilize prices until markets came into rebalance. It is unclear how deep and abiding the alliance between Russia and Saudi Arabia is beyond their current market management arrangement, but the relationship has been accompanied by a deepening of Russian diplomatic and investment activity throughout the Middle East. The second effect on major oil supplying countries is in the area of economic planning and diversification. The most notable example of this is the economic and social reform plan launched in 2016 called Saudi Vision 2030. Through this plan, Saudi Arabia intends to revamp its domestic economy to rely less on oil and diversify its sources of income. Leaving the challenges of implementing this vision aside, it is important to note that many countries that depend on oil-derived revenue to fund their government have taken steps to insulate their economies from periods of sustained low prices. This of course has been done in the

---

[4] Ladislaw, Sarah. "Energy Opportunities in North America." Statement before House Foreign Affairs Subcommittee on Western Hemisphere. 6 June 2017. https://csis-prod.s3.amazonaws.com/s3fs-public/congressional_testimony/ts170607_Ladislaw_testimony_HFAC.pdf%3FVhTcpJ7pb3NmBbAmfyy03YacJg4B6cqL

[5] Tsafos, Nikos. "Europe Turns to Russia, and Elsewhere, to Meet Rising Gas Demand in 2017." 18 January 2018. https://www.csis.org/analysis/europe-turns-russia-and-elsewhere-meet-rising-gas-demand-2017

face of low oil prices so the sustainability of the reforms may be in question when prices rise again, but the reforms were a direct a result of the oil price drop brought on by U.S. oil supply. Notably, countries like Venezuela, once among the largest and most successful oil producing countries in the world, have suffered a great deal under the pressure of lower oil prices after years of neglect and mismanagement under the current and previous leadership.

One often hears it asserted that the increased production of U.S. oil and gas has served to lessen U.S. reliance or entanglement in the Middle East. In fact, this has hardly been the case. The perceived U.S. withdrawal from the Middle East was sparked by a desire to draw down the wartime posture in the Middle East and shift strategic focus to striking a security balance in Asia. The U.S. is no freer of entanglements in the Middle East than it was before the onset of the U.S. oil and gas supply revolution, though it is less concerned about energy security thanks to the low oil prices of the last several years. Following the recent announcement of the U.S. intention to withdraw from the Joint Comprehensive Plan of Action (Iran Agreement), the Trump administration showed that the U.S. still relies on Middle East oil suppliers to help guarantee global price stability in the face of supply disruptions.

As I have written in other publications, energy and foreign policy are often inextricably intertwined, but the ability for policymakers to use energy resources as a tool of targeted foreign policy leverage, or even dominance, is misguided. Very rarely do energy resources alone matter enough to override the many economic, political, security and philosophical disputes that underpin relations between and among countries. Energy can certainly be used as one tool among many to implement a strategy to influence another actor's behavior. Indeed, energy is one of the sectors targeted in our many sanctions regimes against North Korea, Iran, Russia and Venezuela (even when done through financial sanctions). But in each of those cases, the sanctioning of energy investments or resources as part of a broader strategy has yielded mixed and inconclusive results to the crises or stand-offs we face in each country. The U.S. has, however, likely felt freer to sanction other countries with significant energy resources without feeling economic harm in a period of low prices and oversupplied markets.

I recently wrote about some strategies and recommendations for the U.S. to make the most of its energy-advantaged position and use U.S. oil and gas competitiveness to the betterment of the U.S. and global market.[6] First, the United States should continue to support longstanding institutions and arrangements that have served it well over the last several decades. Free trade in energy goods and services is much more in the United States' long-term interest than a purely mercantilist approach to energy deals. It is important to recognize that the United States has a fair number of energy vulnerabilities – related to oil and gas supply disruptions, physical infrastructure protection, and cyber threats. The United States can only be strong if we continue to invest in, and protect

---

[6] Portions of this testimony have been taken from an earlier article Ladislaw, Sarah. "Dissecting the Idea of U.S. Energy Dominance." Oxford Energy Forum, Issue 111, November 2017, Oxford Institute for Energy Studies, https://www.oxfordenergy.org/wpcms/wp-content/uploads/2018/01/OEF-111.pdf

against, those disruptions. The government should think about resilience to physical disruptions like the hurricanes experienced earlier this year. It should contemplate the value of not only its Strategic Petroleum Reserve but of the global system of strategic stocks. Finally, it should devise a strategy for an energy sector that is becoming more and more dependent on digital controls and sensors in the age of cyber warfare.

Second, a truly 'all of the above' approach is warranted if the United States wants to use energy to drive economic growth, job creation, and international competitiveness. The U.S. oil and gas supply surge may get a lot of attention, but the growth in jobs and America's real competitive advantage exists in renewables and other advanced technologies as well. The United States would do well to avoid the promotion of only a certain set of fuels and technologies over others. Developing economies in particular are interested in not only fossil-based energy resources but in distributed solar, wind, storage, microgrids, and a suite of other technologies and services that U.S. companies have to offer.

Third, it is important to understand the value of energy diplomacy. The United States undoubtedly has an energy advantage at its finger tips that can and should be harnessed as much as possible, but it would be a critical mistake to overestimate how much that advantage can be wielded over other countries, or to believe that bilateral trade deals in energy are more important than the fundamental underpinnings of existing trade policy and decades of energy diplomacy in which the U.S. negotiated with other countries using energy as a political tool rather than as a weapon.

The U.S. oil and gas supply revolution has showed us that the more things change the more they stay the same. The U.S. has more economic and security benefits as a result of the increased supply provided by tight oil and shale gas, but it is certainly no panacea for a geopolitically turbulent world to which we are still very much connected.

Mr. POE. Ms. Gross.

## STATEMENT OF MS. SAMANTHA GROSS, FELLOW, CROSS-BROOKINGS INITIATIVE ON ENERGY AND CLIMATE, THE BROOKINGS INSTITUTION

Ms. GROSS. Thank you to Chairman Poe, to Ranking Member Keating, for the invitation to testify today. I am Samantha Gross.

I am a fellow at the Brookings Institution in foreign policy, and my work focusses on energy and environmental geopolitics.

As everyone here has said today, the renaissance in U.S. oil and natural gas production over the past decade has been nothing short of remarkable.

Technological advances unlocked new resources and in 2013 made the U.S. the world's leading producer of petroleum hydrocarbons.

We talk now about peak oil demand, whereas not that long ago in my career we were all focussed on peak oil supply and whether we were going to run out of oil. A big part of that change in attitude has been the change in U.S. production.

Nonetheless, we still import millions of barrels of oil each day at prices set on the global market based on global trends. The United States is not influenced by the ups and downs of global oil prices and how they react to world events.

For example, today's prices at the pump reflect the upcoming reimposition of sanctions on Iran and also Venezuela's plummeting oil production.

Even though we are still a significant net oil importer, growing U.S. oil production has changed the balance of power in the global oil market.

For example, as others have talked about, crude oil prices took a nosedive in late 2014. The average oil price in 2015 and 2016 was less than half of what it had been for the previous 4 years.

OPEC finally decided to act at the end of 2016 to reduce its production and try to push up prices. But in an unprecedented move, it teemed up with Russia to make this happen—a signal of OPEC's declining power and also of the supply glut that growing U.S. production had created.

Unlike for oil, the U.S. is a net exporter of natural gas and has been the world's largest gas producer since 2009. A greater U.S. influence is really more likely to be a gas story than an oil story.

For one reason, natural gas trade differs in important ways from trade in oil. Gas is more difficult to transport and to store, and so expensive infrastructure and long-term contracts also often tie buyers and sellers together.

This less liquid market means that gas sometimes can be more political, as we see in Russian gas trade and the fact that they sometimes have Europe over a barrel with gas pipelines.

Another important reason for the greater influence of gas is that the world is shifting toward natural gas as a preferred fuel. Natural gas has the lowest carbon emissions of any fossil fuel, creates much lower local air pollution than coal, and is a natural partner to renewables in power production since gas-fired power can start up and ramp up and down very quickly in response to changes in renewable energy production and demand.

This global shift toward gas plays into the U.S. strength in natural gas production and can also help move the world toward a lower carbon energy system.

Mexico is, today, the largest consumer of U.S. natural gas and we now, as a result of this trade, have an energy trade surplus with Mexico.

Last year, the value of energy exports to Mexico were more than twice the value of energy imports from Mexico.

As others have mentioned, U.S. LNG is also a supply source that could somewhat reduce Europe's dependence on natural gas from Russia.

Today, U.S. LNG supply is just getting warmed up, and exports to Europe right now are quite small. But the promise of more supply to come, not just from the United States but from others as well, gives Europe a bit more leverage with Russia in terms of natural gas supply.

The U.S. is now a crucial source of global oil and gas supply. But in the middle of this talk about our energy influence, I want us to keep one important thing in mind, and that is that the U.S. energy industry is not structured to use its production toward geopolitical ends.

Unlike the national companies, oil companies of OPEC, the U.S. industry is made up of dozens of companies that make individual investment and production decisions based on profits, not on policy.

The U.S. supply of price-responsive nonpolitical oil and gas contributes to well-functioning global energy markets and reduces the influence of those who want to use their oil and gas supply toward political ends, and this provides a benefit to energy consumers everywhere.

But oil and gas companies generally aren't tools of U.S. foreign policy. We also must remember that the Unites States is a major oil and gas consumer as well as a producer, particularly for oil.

Our energy security depends on the global market. Supply disruptions, as Sarah pointed out, don't just happen abroad. Hurricanes and floods have brought serious disruptions in our domestic energy supply.

Our interconnections with the world and our variety of suppliers are key to U.S. energy security, a source of strength and resilience rather than of weakness.

This concludes my prepared remarks, but I look forward to your questions. Thank you.

[The prepared statement of Ms. Gross follows:]

**Testimony of Samantha Gross[1]**
Fellow, Cross-Brookings Initiative on Energy and Climate, Brookings Institution

**U.S. House of Representatives Committee on Foreign Affairs**
**Subcommittee on Terrorism, Nonproliferation, and Trade**
*Geopolitical Implications of U.S. Oil and Gas Competitiveness in the Global Market*
May 22, 2018

Subcommittee Chair Poe, Ranking Member Keating, and members of the subcommittee, thank you for the invitation to testify today about how growing U.S. oil and gas production affects energy security and trade.

The renaissance in U.S. oil and gas production over the past decade has been nothing short of remarkable. Technological advances unlocked new resources and brought about significant changes in global energy markets. However, we must remember that the United States is a major oil and gas consumer as well. Particularly for oil, our energy security depends on a global market with prices set based on global market conditions. Supply disruptions do not only happen abroad—hurricanes and floods have brought about large disruptions in domestic energy supply. Our interconnections with the world are key to our energy security—a source of strength and resilience, rather than weakness.

The New Energy Abundance

As recently as the mid-2000s, when you heard talk of "peak oil," that meant peak oil supply—the idea that the world was running out of oil. Today that phrase generally means peak oil demand, as new technology, greater efficiency, and concerns about climate change are beginning to move the transportation sector away from oil as a primary fuel. At the same time, advances in oil and gas extraction technology here in the United States have brought online entirely new sources of supply. The combination of long-lateral horizontal wells and hydraulic fracturing led to oil and gas production from resources that had never been economic before. Today we recognize that the oil age won't end because the world ran out of oil.

U.S. oil and gas production has grown tremendously over the last decade. The United States became the world's largest producer of petroleum hydrocarbons in 2013 and has been the world's largest producer of natural gas since 2009. In crude oil production, the United States is in a dead heat with Russia and Saudi Arabia to lead the world.

---

[1] The views expressed in this statement are my own and do not necessarily reflect those of staff members, officers, or trustees of the Brookings Institution.

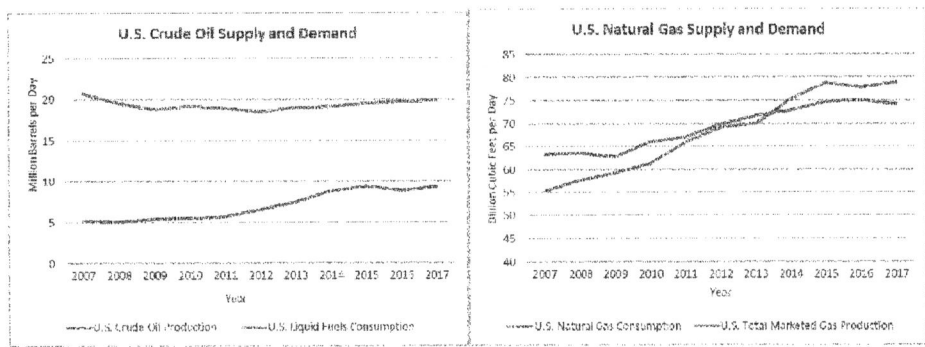

Data Source: U.S. Energy Information Administration

The boom in U.S. oil and natural gas production has brought clear economic benefits, improving our balance of trade and industrial competitiveness, especially in certain industries. For example, the United States is now one of the world's most attractive locations for petrochemical investments, an unthinkable prospect a decade ago.

Even though it is now the among the world's leading oil producers, the United States still imports about 10 million barrels of oil each day. Thus, the United States is not insulated from the ups and downs of the oil price and its reaction to global events. For example, gasoline prices at the pump today reflect the upcoming re-imposition of sanctions on Iran and Venezuela's plummeting oil production.

Recent events demonstrate how the age of abundance and growing U.S. production are changing the balance of power in oil markets. Oil prices stayed above $80 per barrel for four years in 2010 to 2014, an exceptional run of high prices. However, expanding supply caught up with high oil prices and they declined rapidly in late 2014, sinking to as low as $30 per barrel by February of 2016.

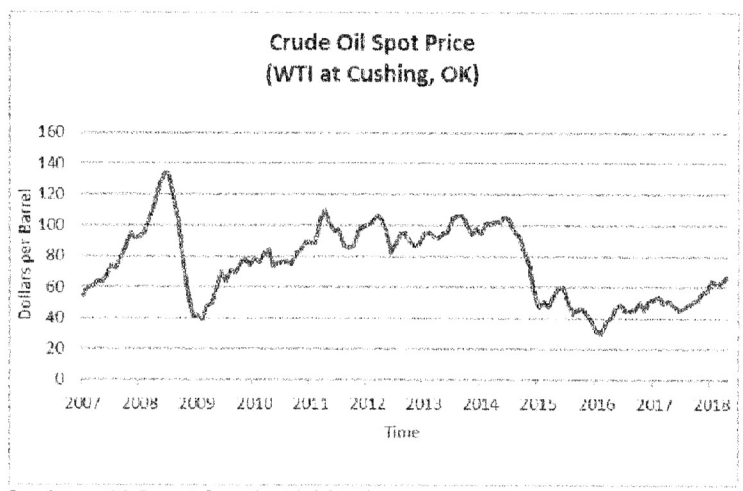

Data Source: U.S. Energy Information Administration

OPEC maintained steady production through the early years of the price collapse. Some argue that OPEC was trying to push U.S. producers out of business by keeping prices low for an extended time; others believe it was more focused on maintaining market share in a well-supplied market. Either way, U.S. producers focused on efficiency and cost reduction and weathered the low-price storm. U.S. production dipped only slightly in 2016 when prices bottomed out.

OPEC changed its strategy at the end of 2016. In an unprecedented move, OPEC teamed up with Russia and a few other oil producers to cut production in an attempt to raise prices and reduce global oil inventories. This strategy was effective and oil prices have risen over the last year and a half. But the need for OPEC to bring Russia into the fold to increase its leverage demonstrates just how much the world has changed. OPEC and Russia have extended their agreement through the end of 2018, but it remains to be seen how long this partnership will hold.

Although growing U.S. oil production has changed the balance of power in oil markets, the U.S. industry is not structured to use its production toward geopolitical ends. Unlike the national oil companies of OPEC, the U.S. industry is made up of dozens of companies that make individual investment and production decisions based on their own costs, financial positions, and appetites for risk. The OPEC producers can work together to move oil prices, an action that would be illegal for U.S. producers under anti-trust laws. Saudi Arabia also holds significant oil production capacity in reserve to deal with oil supply disruptions, an action that would not make economic sense for a for-profit company.

### The Shift toward Natural Gas

Unlike for oil, the United States is a net exporter of natural gas. Our largest natural gas customers are Canada and Mexico, receiving gas through pipelines. Liquefied natural gas, or LNG, is becoming a larger portion of U.S. natural gas exports, reaching 22 percent in 2017. The largest U.S. LNG customers in 2017 included China, South Korea, and Japan in Asia; Mexico and Chile in the Americas; and Spain and Portugal in Europe.

Natural gas trade differs significantly from that for oil. Natural gas is more difficult than oil to transport and store, and for this reason, expensive infrastructure and long-term contracts often tie customers and suppliers together. There is no global natural gas market or price, although growing global LNG supply is beginning to globalize natural gas trade.

In some ways, U.S. natural gas exports can have more geopolitical influence than oil exports. The structure of the U.S. industry is no different—producers make decisions based on profit, not politics—but the nature of natural gas markets, with less fungible supply and the predominance of long-term contracts, makes natural gas trade more inherently political.

Natural gas exports provide clear environmental benefits to our trading partners. Natural gas has the lowest carbon emissions of any fossil fuel and creates much less local air pollution than coal. When used to generate power, natural gas also compliments renewable power sources like wind and solar. Natural gas-fired power can start up quickly and rapidly ramp production up and down in response to changes in wind and solar production, allowing the grid to meet demand at all times. For these reasons, natural gas is becoming a preferred fuel globally, playing into U.S. strength in gas production.

Mexico has become the most important export market for U.S. natural gas, providing benefits on both sides of the border. More than half of 2017 U.S. natural gas exports went to Mexico. We now have a trade surplus with Mexico in energy products—in 2017 the value of energy exports to Mexico was more than twice the value of imports. U.S. natural gas is bringing lower priced and lower carbon electricity for Mexico, along with power system flexibility that allows integration of more renewable power generation.

Additionally, U.S. LNG is one supply source that can reduce Europe's reliance on pipeline gas from Russia. Russian disputes with Ukraine over gas transport in the late 2000s made Russian gas supply to Europe a matter of great concern. Growing LNG supply from the United States and others gives Europeans options, helping them lessen their dependence on Russian gas while still enjoying the benefits of gas as they strive to reduce the carbon emissions from their power supply. U.S. LNG exports are still in the ramp-up phase and exports to Europe (except for the Iberian Peninsula) are tiny today, but the promise of more supply to come strengthens Europe's position.

## Closing Thoughts

The United States has become an indispensable source of oil and gas supply, but the term "energy dominance" is somewhat misleading. To me, "dominance" implies an ability to move markets, whereas the U.S. energy industry, while strong and increasingly important to global energy security, is not structured to achieve that end or other geopolitical goals. U.S. supply of price-responsive, non-political oil and gas contributes to well-functioning global energy markets, providing benefits to energy consumers everywhere.

Mr. POE. I thank all members of the panel. Without objection, the chair will recognize the gentleman from Florida first, Mr. Mast.

Mr. MAST. Thank you, Chairman. I appreciate it.

And Ms. Ladislaw, I wanted to hit you on this but I was also glad to hear you speak about this, Ms. Gross—and I was wondering if you could expand a little bit on what's going on not just with supply disruption—I think we are a little bit more familiar with what that can look like here in the United States of America, but when we branch out and we look at supply disruption in terms of what can happen in Qatar, in Australia, obviously, that you could be looping in the relationship with the proximity of Iran, when we are talking about Qatar but, more specifically, Australia and Russia: What are the natural disaster supply disruptions that we could see, you know, affecting the chains in those places?

Ms. LADISLAW. I will start and then turn it to Sam.

I mean, I think when you look at Australia, it's not a natural disaster supply disruption, but, you know, Australia has a really important example of a story that is meaningful to the U.S.

It built out a huge amount of natural gas export capacity and then experienced a position where their domestic industries were paying prices that were higher than the export markets to which they were selling natural gas, and they had to threaten to curtail natural gas exports from Australia as a result.

And that was just because they weren't able to, you know, expand supplies enough for their domestic market. It was something that took lots and lots of people by surprise. But it harkens back to that midstream infrastructure comment that I brought up before, which is if you have all the gas in the world but if it's in the ground and it can't get to the people that need it, it doesn't do anybody any good.

And so, there's a lot of domestic politics in Australia right now that are really centered around this idea of we've got to make sure we make the domestic market whole as well as be able to, you know, meet our export arrangements.

It's not geopolitical. It's not sexy. It's just business, right? And so I think we—it was probably one of the things that took the U.S. Government so long when it came to exporting LNG facilities here in the U.S. to getting those permits right.

There was a concern here whether their domestic resource base would be adequate for us to support the export of gas and also meet those needs here.

So kind of a wonky logistical issue; one that we seem to have gotten beyond. But Australia thought they got beyond it, too, and then it kind of hit them in the face unexpectedly.

Ms. GROSS. Just a brief comment to that, and that is that there was definitely concern when the Department of Energy was approving—was starting to approve LNG exports that it would push up domestic gas prices.

We haven't seen that thus far. Granted, LNG is just getting warmed up here. But one thing that I think points to the fact that we may get this right is that you see a lot of industries coming back to the United States based on the promise of low gas prices.

In particular, there's been a real renaissance in chemical industry here in the United States. And so they're making significant financial bets on the fact that gas prices in the U.S. will remain quite reasonable.

And so, you know, we'll see what happens. But there's significant money betting that that will go right.

Mr. MAST. Sticking with that same triangle of nations, could you point to any differences on the broad strokes in terms of what creates competitive advantages and disadvantages, based upon environmental regulation for the—for the refinement and the production of natural gas rather than mining? Thank you.

Ms. LADISLAW. In those three countries?

Mr. MAST. Yes. Australia, Russia——

Ms. LADISLAW. So this is a good question. I am not sure I've got the best answer for what creates competitive advantages. All three economies function very differently in terms of how they pursue both domestic gas production, export, and investment for petrochemicals.

I think one of the interesting things is for a long time both Russia and Qatar functioned as the least cost producers of gas with a readily available resource base and, therefore, they had a natural advantage to refining in petrochemical industries in terms of what they were able to invest.

The U.S. has been able to do a heck of a lot more of that business in recent years as a result of that. In terms of environmental permitting, I really can't speak to that issue.

Mr. MAST. Does anybody on the panel have anything to offer in terms of broad stroke differences between environmental permitting across those nations?

I will take that. Yes, sir.

Mr. CARROLL. Yes. I would just say that in the case of Russia in particular, I think the lack of available data, especially with regard to environmental impact, methane emissions, and the like is a little more suspect and a little less available.

That said, some of the major producers are working to mitigate those emissions is one example.

Mr. MAST. Thank you.

The chair will now yield back. Thanks for the time.

Mr. POE. I thank the gentleman from Florida.

The chair recognizes the gentleman from the Republic of Massachusetts, Mr. Keating.

Mr. KEATING. Thank you, Mr. Chairman.

I am sorry for your loss, Dr. Medlock.

The overall rosy picture—before I get into international issues, a quick domestic question, though. The impression was the U.S. is going to be in a great position, flowing with cheaper, cleaner energy.

But there are portions of the United States that may not have as rosy a forecast. Now, where I am in Massachusetts, sometimes the access issues become difficult, and we faced some problems there.

Are there other parts of the country, and how does a place like that cope with those problems?

Dr. Carroll, do you want to start?

Mr. CARROLL. The first thing you did this winter was get a ship of LNG in from Russia from the Amal plant, which helped deal with the—in order to keep your heat going and your power being generated there.

That's, clearly, as I look across the United States, the biggest constraint in pipeline capacity is in that New England-New York area, which constrains the flow of gas both into the northeastern U.S. and eastern Canada as well.

And it's a shame, given the huge quantities of affordable gas that are located in Marcellus just a couple hundred miles away.

So as I see it, that would be a critical—a critical opportunity to increase the infrastructure. That said, how do you get around it today? You could import, as you did with LNG through the Everett Terminal in Massachusetts.

You can, of course, move more toward renewables as best you can to minimize the demand for fossil fuels. But as, again, I look across the country, that pinch point up there is probably the most acute.

Mr. KEATING. And they're closing—decommissioning a nuclear plant there, too.

So anyone else have anything to add about the U.S. difficulties?

Mr. MEDLOCK. Thank you for the question, and I think this actually brings up a good opportunity to draw out a parallel that Sarah actually just raised with regard to Australia.

The very high natural gas prices they experienced in the state of South Australia in Victoria were the result of a lack of sufficient pipeline capacity to move gas from where it's produced to where it was needed.

That is something that will happen in perpetuity until either capacity is added or storage options are added in the region, and I've had some conversations with the foreign minister there about this. They're looking at all of those issues.

The thing that they run into constantly, though, is local opposition to anything related to fossil fuels. And so they continue to push back on anything until the price jumps and then they realize, well, this isn't really a viable option, and it's led to some interest in developing floating re-gas capability to back door—the end of pipe constraint that exists to access those markets.

In a lot of ways, that's what Everett serves currently in the New England market. It serves as a way to sort of back door that end of pipe market when you have demand rise because it gets very cold, for example.

Interestingly, as was just pointed out, this past winter we saw a cargo of Russian LNG that was reloaded in the U.K. land in Boston and I know that got some people's hairs on edge, right?

Mr. KEATING. It didn't affect me, though. [Laughter.]

Mr. MEDLOCK. Well, no, but——

Mr. KEATING. But if I could—I am running out of time—just want to ask one international kind of question. We use sanctions a great deal in our country now with major oil and gas-producing countries like Iran, Russia, Venezuela.

How is that working, and what are the effects of that? I know Ms. Ladislaw mentioned that, but particularly the other three panelists, or we can hear more from Ms. Ladislaw.

Ms. GROSS. It depends on which sanctions and where. I will say that the sanctions that we are putting back in place on Iran will be quite effective.

The reason why these sanctions are so effective or will be so effective is that they're focused on the U.S. banking system, and so you can't clear Iranian oil or gas through the U.S. banking system.

Given that—given that the dollar is the reserve currency—that oil trade happens in dollars—that makes it extremely difficult for them to sell abroad.

And so that sort of sanction is extremely difficult to get around. You may see it some, particularly with respect to the Chinese, who can do some trade without doing—without using dollars.

But I think those sanctions will be incredibly effective in cutting exports from Iran.

Ms. LADISLAW. I think financial and energy sector related sanctions have been very effective when they're implemented multilaterally because it doesn't just make the, you know, sort of air from this part of the balloon go to some other place, right, which happens with oil, quite typically.

I think the longer-term issue is what's the long-term consequence for a intensely global industry that has to deal with—I don't know when Russian energy sanctions or financial sanctions will ever go away.

I don't see an end to that. And so countries around the world are looking for ways to work around them and so it's creating a whole different sort of alternative in financing and technology and a whole bunch of other things for countries that would really just like to stay away from our ability to reach them.

It's a long-term problem, but I do think it's one that we've got to keep on the horizon, particularly when we don't know when the sanctions will go away.

Mr. KEATING. My time has expired. I yield back.

Mr. POE. I thank the gentleman.

Once again, I thank all of you for being here. I have the philosophy I am for everything below the ground and everything above the ground. I am for all of the above and below.

We haven't talked about several of those, like renewables and wind power, solar energy. We'll do that at a later hearing.

When I was in India and talked to the foreign minister there, the foreign minister kept saying 1,300,000,000 people, and finally it dawned on me that there's 1 billion more people in India than there are in the United States.

That's a lot of folks, and I think I saw every one of them when I was over there. The conversation was about getting LNG from the United States to India.

We can set an—and I agree with you, the United States looks at energy differently because these companies are all in the business to make a profit—capitalism, if we can use that word—as opposed to nationalized energy companies.

But it does have the geopolitical effect, as well—as—maybe not the primary objective, but it does have that objective.

And so can you highlight for me selling natural gas where we are with India? My understanding is we can develop it, produce it, send it across the ocean, and sell it to them and they can buy it cheaper than they can drill it themselves, and we still make a profit.

So where is that going? Dr. Medlock, do you want to comment on that?

Mr. MEDLOCK. I would be happy to. Thanks for the question.

I think you're touching on something that's actually bigger than just India. Currently, when we have discussions about geopolitical influence of the U.S. energy renaissance, we tend to want to focus on what's happening in Europe with regard to Russia because that's sort of the thing that's hot button—that's very relevant right now.

But if we put a longer-term view on this, you quickly come to the realization that if I just put my hands on a map around China, India, and the ASEAN countries, that's 3 billion people in a part of the world that's growing at a clip of greater than 5 percent a year.

So for the next 20, 30, years, that is the engine that's going to drive the shape of the energy landscape globally. The better we could connect with rulers in that part of the world, with industries in that part of the world, with individuals in that part of the world, the more influence we'll actually be able to have over the—over how that sort of all those geopolitical relationships ultimately shake out.

That will actually convey tremendous benefit to the U.S. Government and its people, quite frankly, as we go forward over the next two to three decades.

Moving beyond that, we still haven't even touched on, if we are going to do the math, another 3.3 billion people that live in sub-Saharan Africa, Latin America, Central Asia, and the Middle East.

You're talking about a massive number of people outside of where we conventionally talk about, or traditionally talk about trading oil and natural gas that we have the ability to reach and make contact with—again, to shape and influence discussions around energy, around foreign policy, et cetera.

And energy is a great way to do that because energy is the go of things, to steal a quote. It is the thing that drives economic engines around the world and it will always be the case, regardless of the form of energy. It's always going to be important.

Mr. POE. I recently met with the Speakers of the House of Ukraine and Moldova and Georgia, and they are working together to move more to the West, to democracy, et cetera.

What is—what is the United States doing energy wise for those three specific countries? Anything?

Or are they developing their own resources? Are we selling them our fuel? Does anyone want to comment on those three specific countries?

Ms. LADISLAW. I don't know each of them individually in a great deal of detail. My understanding is the strategy is threefold.

One is to sort of help with the internal governance, particularly in Ukraine, of their domestic energy system, which has been sort of fraught with oh, gosh, a whole bunch of different problems.

Two, is to make sure the interconnections in the market within Europe is as efficient as possible and can work those countries into the system, and then the third is dealing with Russia vis-a-vis energy supplies into Europe and making sure that they have sort of a level playing field for negotiating prices. I can't speak too much beyond that, though.

Mr. POE. Dr. Medlock.

Mr. MEDLOCK. Yes, let me add one thing to that.

I think the strategy really has been one of trying to promote a different type of governance around markets that allow for more flexibility in the delivery of different types of supply.

So this, ultimately, allows for this credible threat hypothesis that I mentioned earlier to be realized in Europe. So this gets to liberalization of markets—you know, actually seeing price signals that are transmitted across the European continent that allow for expansion of pipeline capacity, connecting different points of entry into the continent, allowing back haul services to move from Western to Central to Eastern Europe, which didn't exist really to any extent just a decade ago.

All these sorts of things have actually allowed more flexibility and fungibility of gas molecules in the European market, and that's really the best you can do absent a direct point of contact.

The Ukraine—there's no ability to import LNG into the Ukraine. So U.S. gas isn't going to land there unless it lands in India and moves via back haul by pipeline.

Same thing with Moldova, Romania—you name all those countries that are sort of blocked, right. It's a similar sort of issue.

So it really is about altering market structure and conveying the advantages that a different market structure will actually bring in terms of providing energy security, and this is fundamentally a trade question.

Mr. POE. The—I think Mexico and United States and Canada are intertwined dramatically in the energy field. Dr. Medlock, there's a small business guy in Houston that has all of—he's a manufacturer. He's an assembler.

He has all those little parts made in Mexico that are brought in to his business in Houston. He assembles them, then he sends them out to the Houston ship channel. Of course, we get fuel from Canada as well.

Let me hear just what all four of you think on this basic concept of—we can call it free trade—regarding energy and energy supply—this energy supply chain.

Do you think it's a good idea? Do you think—what do we need to do to make it better for our economy?

Each one of you can comment on it. All right. Mr. Carroll, we'll start with you.

Mr. CARROLL. I will just put it in perspective from the natural gas side throughout North America.

If you look at it as a—as a unit, we get about seven—look at U.S. demand. About 7 percent of that is actually imported from Canada.

There's a net on that in terms of we send them some, they send us some. And about 7 percent of our production goes to Mexico.

So it's—you can look at it as 93 percent of what we produce, we consume. But there is some movement between the continents and, it's—the integrated North American market I can tell you is the envy of the world.

So there's a—there's a lot of power and competitive advantage based on the way that mechanism works.

Ms. LADISLAW. Yes, I think——

Mr. POE. Ms. Ladislaw.

Ms. LADISLAW [continuing]. The super boring issue of sort of standards and policy harmonization, which has always been kind of boring for, you know, from a policy perspective. It's something we can continue to do, particularly as we are inventing new technologies and digitalization within the electric power sector.

All of these things we have mechanisms—trilateral mechanisms between all three countries to be able to do that. I just think we need to continue to do those things.

I see more threats to the integrated North American economy from the way that we are approaching the NAFTA trade arrangement right now but also from steel tariffs and other things that are, broadly, discouraging for companies that really would like to have a North American frame of mind.

The other big threat is actually one that Representative Keating brought up, which is that infrastructure is challenging in all three countries right now. I think what we need to do is look at particular places like the Gulf Coast area or the Northeast or even, you know, the West Coast where we've got really big advantages from a resource space or from a technology and innovation standpoint and try and build kind of regional innovation hubs, regional energy hubs, where we understand how the infrastructure and the educational and university environment and the business environment all sort of paddle in the same direction toward really making the most of those advantages. I just don't think we've thought that way yet.

Mr. POE. Ms. Gross.

Ms. GROSS. I agree with everything the folks to the right—to the right of me have said, but I will add just an additional point. It's really also a no-brainer.

It's a no-brainer from a trade and economic perspective. It's also a no-brainer from an environmental perspective.

Any time you're taking these products and shipping them to nearby markets, that's a real advantage. You're also allowing Mexico to take advantage of the significant natural gas reserves that we had here.

The Mexican energy sector has significantly restructured recently and allowed much more outside participation. It's bringing more renewable energy, and the gas is a fantastic partner for that.

And so not only is this good for the United States, good for—you know, good to have a regional energy system, it's also good from an environmental perspective. I think we can give it two thumbs up from any number of points of view.

Mr. POE. Dr. Medlock.

Mr. MEDLOCK. I think Sarah's points are fantastic, actually. The integrated nature of the North American market conveys massive amounts of opportunity both on the environmental front and the commercial front.

Commercially, you connect markets, you connect consumers with producers, you actually make those transactions lower cost, which actually helps grown businesses. It does all sorts of things that are fabulous for job creation, wealth creation, et cetera, on both sides of the border.

Environmentally, you have actually seen in Mexico—and Sam was just referring to this—you have seen in Mexico a reduction in fuel oil use in power generation.

Why is that? Well, it's because you have got a low—you have got low cost natural gas that's being produced just north of the border and it's moving south and it's being put into natural gas-combined cycle generation facilities and it's allowing Mexicans to actually reap the benefits of the North American gas boom just like we do in Texas, just like we do in Massachusetts, just like we do anywhere.

So those types of benefits actually when they're conveyed broadly as a result of trade that can actually occur unimpeded are tremendous on both commercial and environmental fronts.

Mr. POE. Well, thank you all. I appreciate your being here and also your expertise. It's fascinating to have all of you all here to enlighten us about the way things really are. So it's very good.

Thank you, and this subcommittee is adjourned.

Thank you.

[Whereupon, at 3:04 p.m., the committee was adjourned.]

# APPENDIX

Material Submitted for the Record

## SUBCOMMITTEE HEARING NOTICE
## COMMITTEE ON FOREIGN AFFAIRS
U.S. HOUSE OF REPRESENTATIVES
WASHINGTON, DC 20515-6128

### Subcommittee on Terrorism, Nonproliferation, and Trade
### Ted Poe (R-TX), Chairman

**TO:** MEMBERS OF THE COMMITTEE ON FOREIGN AFFAIRS

You are respectfully requested to attend an OPEN hearing of the Committee on Foreign Affairs to be held by the Subcommittee on Terrorism, Nonproliferation, and Trade in Room 2200 of the Rayburn House Office Building (and available live on the Committee website at http://www.ForeignAffairs.house.gov):

**DATE:** Tuesday, May 22, 2018

**TIME:** 2:00 p.m.

**SUBJECT:** Geopolitics of U.S. Oil and Gas Competitiveness

**WITNESSES:** Kenneth B. Medlock III, Ph.D.
Senior Director
Center for Energy Studies
Baker Institute for Public Policy
Rice University

Mr. David Carroll
President and Chief Executive Officer
Gas Technology Institute

Ms. Sarah Ladislaw
Director and Senior Fellow
Energy and National Security Program
Center for Strategic and International Studies

Ms. Samantha Gross
Fellow
Cross-Brookings Initiative on Energy and Climate
The Brookings Institution

### By Direction of the Chairman

*The Committee on Foreign Affairs seeks to make its facilities accessible to persons with disabilities. If you are in need of special accommodations, please call 202/225-5021 at least four business days in advance of the event, whenever practicable. Questions with regard to special accommodations in general (including availability of Committee materials in alternative formats and assistive listening devices) may be directed to the Committee.*

## COMMITTEE ON FOREIGN AFFAIRS

MINUTES OF SUBCOMMITTEE ON _Terrorism, Nonproliferation, and Trade_ HEARING

Day __Tuesday__ Date __05/22/2018__ Room __2200__

Starting Time __2:00pm__ Ending Time __3:05pm__

Recesses ____ (___to___)(___to___)(___to___)(___to___)(___to___)(___to___)

**Presiding Member(s)**
*Representative Poe*

*Check all of the following that apply:*

Open Session ☑
Executive (closed) Session ☐
Televised ☐

Electronically Recorded (taped) ☑
Stenographic Record ☑

**TITLE OF HEARING:**
*"Geopolitics of U.S. Oil and Gas Competitiveness"*

**SUBCOMMITTEE MEMBERS PRESENT:**
*Rep. Poe, Keating, Perry, Schneider, Zeldin, Mast*

**NON-SUBCOMMITTEE MEMBERS PRESENT:** *(Mark with an * if they are not members of full committee.)*
*Rohrabacher*

**HEARING WITNESSES:** Same as meeting notice attached? Yes ☑ No ☐
*(If "no", please list below and include title, agency, department, or organization.)*

**STATEMENTS FOR THE RECORD:** *(List any statements submitted for the record.)*

TIME SCHEDULED TO RECONVENE _____
or
TIME ADJOURNED __3:05pm__

Subcommittee Staff Associate

www.ingramcontent.com/pod-product-compliance
Lightning Source LLC
Chambersburg PA
CBHW062341220526
45469CB00008B/2796